365 WAYS TO SAVE MONEY

Also by Lucy H. Hedrick

365 Ways to Save Time
365 Ways to Save Time with Kids
Five Days to an Organized Life

365 WAYS TO SAVE MONEY

Lucy H. Hedrick

Hearst Books
New York

The ideas and suggestions in this book are not intended to substitute for the help and services of a trained professional. Matters regarding your finances may require financial consultation and supervision, and following any of the suggestions in this book should be done in conjunction with the services of a qualified financial professional.

Copyright © 1994 by Lucy H. Hedrick

ISBN 0-688-12701-0

Printed in the United States of America

For Tom Mullen

ACKNOWLEDGMENTS

I'm grateful for money-saving suggestions from many friends, but most especially from:

Mr. William E. Bausch
Computer Consultant

Ms. Paulette Ensign
Organizing Solutions, Inc.

Mr. Christopher W. Beale, CFP
Financial Planner

Ms. Jackie Hammock
Real Estate Agent

Ms. Christine Begole
Electronics/Technology Writer

Ms. Lois Herbst
Checks & Balances, Etc.

Mr. Albert B. Brodbeck, CLU
Insurance

Ms. Frankie Hollister, CFA
Portfolio Manager

Mr. Roger R. Cucci
Special Agent

Ms. Robin Loughman
Writer/Editor

Acknowledgments

Ms. Nancy McConnell
Real Estate Agent

Ms. Judy Margolin
Author

Mr. Peter Mullen
Investment Counselor

Ms. Lee Paine
Photographer/Writer

Ms. Carol Purse
Interior Decorator

Mr. Charles Reich
Author

Ms. Sandy Soule
Travel Writer

Mr. Guy Stretton, CPA
Accountant

Mr. Alan Weiss, CFP, CPA,
PFS
Financial Planner

Mr. Steven S. Wortman, CPA
Accountant

CONTENTS

Contents

INTRODUCTION

One day a friend remarked to me, "You know, Lucy, people can save a lot of money if they're organized."

True, I thought. As the author of three books on saving time and getting organized, I recognize that by knowing where to get information, asking the right questions, and planning ahead, you can avoid costly mistakes. Furthermore, as I work with my clients on their productivity, I focus on the direct connection between effective time management and making, or saving, money.

With hands-on experience managing my own resources, I've dealt extensively with financial experts, so I decided to assemble a collection of ideas for saving money that would not consume a lot of time.

365 Ways to Save Money tells you how to reduce spending, get a better return on the assets you've accumulated, and pay

Introduction

less in taxes. If you want to delegate your money managing, you'll read about ways to do that. You'll also find many toll-free telephone numbers that will reduce your research time.

I hope you enjoy the tips and you find many that will work to your economic advantage!

365 WAYS TO SAVE MONEY

BANKING

1

If you write a lot of checks every month, ordering them directly
from a printer rather than purchasing them through your bank
will save you money. Your bank may charge you more than
$12.00 for two hundred plain checks printed with your name
and address. The same number of checks ordered directly from
a printer cost just $4.95. Two reliable companies to purchase
checks from are Checks in the Mail (800-733-4443) and Cur-
rents, Inc. (800-426-0822).

2

Almost everyone has heard the admonishment, "To accumulate
savings, pay your savings vehicle a fixed amount once a month
when you pay your other bills." However, if you think you'll

forget (or deliberately skip a month or two), arrange for your bank to automatically transfer a set amount from your checking account into savings. (Note: With any fixed instructions to your bank, it's necessary to monitor your balance to prevent overdraft charges.)

3

Many people choose the convenience of doing all their banking—checking, saving, mortgage, auto loan, charge cards, etc.—at one bank, but that doesn't necessarily save you money. Since most banking today is handled by mail or by phone, you'll get better rates if you shop around for the best deals.

4

If your interest-paying checking account falls below the required minimum, banks often charge a hefty fee that can quickly eat up and even exceed the interest you earn. Unless you're comfortable maintaining a high minimum balance in your checking account, choose a no-interest plan. (Furthermore, if you put your former minimum balance into a savings plan, you'll probably net more profit, after fees, than you would have from the low-interest checking. Take the time to do the math to see if you're ahead of the game.)

Pay attention to what your bank charges for automated teller machine (ATM) withdrawals. Twenty-five cents at your own branch is one thing, but some banks charge a much higher price for an ATM transaction at another bank that networks with yours.

6

Sometimes you can find totally free checking if you write very few—typically, six or fewer—checks each month. But that means six checks posted to your account. Someone who deposits your check late could cause you to pay a penalty for going over the minimum number.

7

If you deposit more than $5,000 in a single day from a bank outside your Federal Reserve district, your bank has the right to hold the funds in excess of $5,000 for up to eleven business days. Deposits of less than $5,000 must be made available within five business days.

8

If your salary is paid, or credited, by direct deposit, some banks will waive some of their fees. If you can live without canceled checks, look into cheaper checking accounts that return an image of your checks or simply a list of them.

9

You don't have to live near your savings bank. You can find high-savings-rate banks, which generally pay 1 percent above the national average, by subscribing to the newsletter, *100 Highest Yields*. A two-month trial subscription, which also lists the banks' safety ratings, costs $34. Send your payment to *100 Highest Yields*, Box 088888, North Palm Beach, FL 33408. For more information, call 407-627-7330.

10

If you buy a certificate of deposit (CD) from a bank, pay attention to the warning of "penalty for early withdrawal." Penalties are usually one to three months of interest, but if you withdraw your money after one month, the other two months will be subtracted from your principal.

Are you discouraged by the low interest your bank is paying on certificates of deposit (CDs)? You'll get a better return if you put your money away for a longer term. At this writing, five-year CDs are paying an average of 4.76 percent, compared to 2.95 percent for one-year CDs and 1.92 percent on money-market accounts.

As an alternative to banks, credit unions are a good idea because they usually charge less for consumer loans and pay more on savings than other financial institutions. They used to be available through your employer and you could arrange to have a fixed amount deducted from your paycheck and deposited into the credit union, but now even self-employed and small-business people can participate. Call the credit unions listed in your Yellow Pages and ask about membership requirements. You can also write to the Credit Union National Association, Box 431, Madison, WI 53701, or call them at 800-358-5710. They'll give you the address of your state association and tell you which local credit unions you may be eligible to join.

CAMERAS

13

Professional photographers will tell you that they take many black-and-white photos to a achieve a few good shots. And rather than having their developer make a print of all of them, they request a "proof sheet," which shows all the pictures in negative size, allowing them to choose the specific photos they want to print. This is much less expensive than printing a copy of each photo and then throwing away the duds.

14

The new disposable cameras offer many advantages: They use 35mm film, and they're lighter to carry, inexpensive (approximately $9 for a bare-bones variety), and great for kids to use or to take on vacation. However, buy one in your hometown rather than at your vacation destination. Tourist and resort areas invariably charge too much.

15

Unless you're a professional photographer, take advantage of low-cost private-label camera film. Retail chains like Kmart and Target feature their own brand of 35mm film (made by the 3M Company and others), which costs 25 percent less than Kodak or Fuji.

CARS

16

There's a lot of money to be saved if you buy a European car in Europe. Prerequisite: You have to travel to the country where the car is made. However, this so-called "European delivery plan" is arranged at a U.S. dealer. Danielle, a music teacher accompanying a student orchestra to Scandinavia, went to the Saab factory. She explains: "I paid my money here, filled out the papers there, and the Saab factory shipped my new car to my U.S. dealer." Danielle's savings: She would have had to pay $2,500 more for her car at a U.S. dealer (and her savings more than paid for the cost of her trip!).

Always figure resale value in your car-buying equation. Assuming it has been maintained and regularly serviced, what is your car going to be worth as a trade-in, or for sale by owner, in three years? In five years? Certain features—a power sunroof, for example, which costs a little more up front—will add $400–$500 to the resale value, depending on your make and model. For information on specific enhancements, consult the *National Automobile Dealers Association (NADA) Official Used Car Guide* ("The Blue Book") available at your public library.

18

Paying cash for, as opposed to financing, a new car is generally the most cost-effective payment method because you don't have to pay interest (assuming that the car-loan interest is greater than what your cash is earning in investments). Also, some dealers take more off their price if you're going to pay cash (or finance through their agencies). However, if you own your own company and use your automobile as part of conducting your business, it may be more prudent to finance your car purchase because interest on business loans is deductible. Check with your accountant.

19

The automobile press loves to compare performance data such as the time it takes a car to go from zero to sixty miles per hour. As a shopper, you'll save money if you pay attention to a less-touted statistic: the time required for stopping, from sixty to zero miles per hour. In addition to the superior safety of cars that stop more quickly, fewer collisions mean you won't eat into your insurance deductible, nor do you face the increased premiums that so often follow accidents.

20

You must consider the implications of new-car sales tax when pricing your old car to sell it privately. For example, if you buy a new car for $24,000 and the dealer will give you $4,000 for your old car, $20,000 plus, say, 6 percent sales tax ($1,200) gives you a total cost of $21,200. Without the trade-in, your cost is $24,000 plus 6 percent sales tax ($1,440), or $25,440. Therefore, your break-even point on a private sale is $4,240.

21

A prospective buyer's perception of your four-to-five-year-old car will be greatly influenced by all painted surfaces. The buyer will project the maintenance of the car's exterior to re-

flect the condition of the motor, drive train, etc. Here's a re-
alistic scenario: If a fully loaded, high-performance sedan costs
$25,000 new, after five years, it should be worth 40 percent
of the purchase price, or $10,000. However, if the exterior
paint surfaces aren't good, your sedan will be worth maybe 30
percent of the purchase price, or $7,500. That's a $2,500 loss
in value.

22

If you have taken care of your car, you're probably going to
be able to get more money if you sell it yourself (provided
you have the time to handle the phone inquiries and show the
car). It's also a double win because dealers generally will give
you a better purchase price if they don't have to accept your
trade-in.

23

When researching car options and shopping around, pay attention to a car's energy costs. Assume that you're going to pay
more at the gasoline pump in the coming years as more and
more areas are required to sell cleaner but costlier gasoline,
and as more states increase gasoline taxes. However, no matter
what gas costs or how far you drive, a higher miles-per-gallon
figure saves you money. Take the EPA's mileage estimate and
apply it to the approximate number of miles you drive in a
year. For example:

12,000 mi/yr (EPA) 20 mi/gal = 600 gal @ \$1.30 = \$ 780/yr
@ \$1.70 = \$1,020/yr

(EPA) 25 mi/gal = 480 gal @ \$1.30 = \$ 624/yr
@ \$1.70 = \$ 816/yr

(EPA) 30 mi/gal = 400 gal @ \$1.30 = \$ 520/yr
@ \$1.70 = \$ 680/yr

24

My friend Bob tells me people are "penny-wise and pound foolish" when they buy cars. He sees a lot of people drive to another dealer far away, just to save \$50. "The better procedure is to visit an out-of-town dealer *first* so you can become a seasoned, knowledgeable buyer. Learn how the manufacturer is shipping the cars and what are the standard versus the add-on features. Then visit your target dealer(s) closer to home."

25

In the mid-1990s, there will be a problem with automobile air conditioners. Cars have been using a refrigerant known as R-12, or Freon, which is now being phased out to help the environment. New regulations under the Clean Air Act require new cars, starting in the 1995 model year, to use R-134a systems. What does this mean to your pocketbook? You won't be

able to find any more R-12, and what you do find will be pro-
hibitively expensive, and the new R-134a product will destroy
the air-conditioning systems in older cars.

26

Cars often drop in price and dealers become more willing to
negotiate later in the model year. Also, you're more likely to
get a good price if you shop at the end of the month because
dealers don't want to carry their inventory into the next month.
Check the manufacturer's label on the driver's-side doorpost to
see when the car was made. If it's been sitting on the lot for a
while, you're in a better position to bargain.

27

Do you have limited time? Do you hate haggling over price?
Maybe you should sign on with a car-shopping service. In most
cases, after joining the service for a fee, you fill out a form
describing the specific model you want. Then the service lo-
cates a dealer carrying your desired car and charges you less
than sticker price. Look in the Yellow Pages under "Buyers'
Services," or in the automotive press.

28

The Vehicle Information Network is a toll-free number that lists used cars for sale in a caller's area. Dealers pay $795 a month to advertise; an individual pays $29.95 to list a car. Buyers receive, at no charge, a list of available cars, according to the year, make, color, and mileage specifications that they're looking for. The number is 800-227-7327.

29

General Motors Saturn dealers have been selling cars at their "no-dicker sticker" prices, and the company sold more cars per dealer in 1991 than any other manufacturer. This new, no-haggle technique is catching on with other dealers, but consumers should still shop around. Another dealer may be selling the same car at a lower "sticker price."

30

Look for a car model whose price is down from its previous level. Many companies have cut prices on slow sellers. For example, Ford cut the price of its Thunderbird LX an incredible 20 percent.

31

Look for cash rebates. You won't find many on Japanese makes, but several popular domestic cars carry generous rebates.

32

"To qualify as a skilled car bargainer, know the exact model and options you want before you start dickering," says Jerry Edgerton in *Money* magazine. "Try to pay 3 percent to 4 percent over cost—not counting rebates or dealer incentives—for a car priced under $20,000, and 5 percent to 7 percent over for higher-priced luxury models."

33

I realized every time my service station added oil or windshield-wiper fluid to my car, the cost seemed higher than it would have if I had serviced the vehicle on my own. Now, I purchase oil and fluid by the case at an auto or discount store and add it myself. I also save money by pumping my own gas and paying cash.

34

Once you identify automobiles that meet your price, style, function, and performance criteria, focus on quality. The J. D. Power Survey provides quality data measured in problems per one hundred cars. The best models belong to the "Under 100 Club." (Note: In 1993, Japanese and American manufacturers produced equal numbers of such cars.) The cost of your new car up front is one thing, but your costs for maintenance, repairs, or problems later also have to be figured into your budget. Watch for the results from the J. D. Power Survey in your daily newspaper or in the automotive press.

35

Sometimes you will find the lowest rates for car loans through your credit union—as much as two percentage points lower than other lenders. One caveat: Make sure the credit union displays a National Credit Union Administration (NCUA) sticker, which tells you its deposits are federally insured.

36

If you own your own home, home-equity loans are often unbeatable as a way to finance major purchases, including automobiles. Interest rates can be significantly lower than those you would pay for other consumer loans, and the interest you pay is deductible, as long as the home-equity loan is for $100,000 or less.

37

Just as with appliances, the experts say nix to extended service contracts for new cars. Contracts typically cost $600 to $2,000 for two to five years of coverage, but the big-ticket items covered by the policy rarely give buyers trouble during the first few years of ownership. (An exception might occur if you buy a used car manufactured before 1993. An extended warranty will cost less than the price of replacing your old air-conditioning system. See tip number 25.)

38

Increasingly, car shoppers pay as much attention to the performance characteristics of an automobile's sound equipment as its power train. That's fine, but it's a good idea to consider the risks associated with high-end car stereos. It can be both expensive and demoralizing to endure the broken glass and console damage that come with losing enticing automobile CD and tape players to local hoodlums.

39

Jack, who owns a profitable car dealership, advises, "If you want to reduce your risk of audio theft, get your car stereo factory installed at the time of purchase. A stereo unit added as an afterthought is an invitation to a thief."

40

Mark, owner of a custom audio store, says car owners can deter thieves by choosing a stereo receiver with a computer chip that renders the stereo useless in any vehicle other than the one in which it was originally installed.

41

Some older car models have a Benzi box; that is, a removable sleeve unit, which allows the owner to easily slip a car stereo in or out of the dashboard or console. Many newer cars are now equipped with a removable face unit, a lightweight cover to the car stereo, which the owner can simply carry away in his pocket. (This face unit has a serial number which must match the number on its stereo for the unit to function.)

Are you turned off by the cost of an automobile alarm system? Install a lower-priced dummy system consisting of several small flashing lights. "If a thief sees a car with flashing lights next to a car without lights, he's going to break into the one that's not flashing," says my friend Mike, a police officer.

To lease or buy, that is the question. The answer? It depends. And you have to look at more than just the surface numbers. Monthly lease payments are almost always less than monthly loan installments for the same car. However, if you want to get out of your lease early, you'll pay dearly and have no car to take with you. Study carefully the "early termination" provisions of any lease you consider.

COLLEGE

44

If you or your child is applying for scholarship money to attend college, look for money for tuition and course-related expenses (books, supplies, and equipment), which is not taxable to you as long as you (or your child) are working toward a degree. If you need scholarship money for room and board and incidental expenses, you can of course seek it out, but know that it is considered taxable income.

45

When looking for financial aid from sources other than the college of your choice, be aware that many colleges will subtract this outside aid from the package that you're getting. *Be-*

College

fore your son or daughter looks for and applies for scholarships, ask a financial-aid officer at each college you're considering how the school treats outside awards.

46

In determining a student's eligibility for scholarships, financial-aid programs look first at the student's assets and income, and then at the parents' income. To increase your eligibility, realize capital gains before January of your child's junior year in high school or postpone them until after his or her junior year in college. The same goes for any bonuses or other lump sums whose timing you can control.

47

Conventional advice, when saving for college expenses, is to invest in a child's name so that earnings are taxed in the child's bracket. But families that would end up qualifying for significant aid—particularly grants—lose out on aid by having saved in the child's name—even after the tax benefits are taken into account. If you expect to qualify for more than token aid, put savings in your own name.

48

According to Judy Margolin, author of *Financing a College Education: The Essential Guide for the '90s*, tuition costs at colleges that are very highly endowed are generally less than those of institutions with a smaller endowment. In addition, geography can play a part in college costs (southern schools tend to be less expensive), as can the type of school (your state and community colleges cost less than private schools).

49

College-bound children of middle- and upper-income parents who don't qualify for financial aid can reduce college costs by getting merit scholarships. Colleges do this to attract top students. Take, for example, the Merit Award Program at Goucher College, in Towson, Maryland (800-638-4278). Up-to-the-minute information on more than four thousand grant and scholarship opportunities can be found in *Cash for College*, by Cynthia and Phillip McKee, published by Hearst Books.

50

Starting with the 1993–1994 school year, anyone, regardless of need, can enroll in the federal student-aid program. There are three categories: basic student (Stafford or Perkins) loans, SLS loans for students who are *not* dependent on their parents, and PLUS loans for parents. Interest rates are lower than those of the old programs, and for the first time, loans are available for part-time students. After you are accepted by a college or an accredited trade school, apply for your loan through the school's financial aid office.

51

Work/study programs are a very viable alternative when you are considering how to pay for a college education. More than nine hundred public and private schools offer "cooperative education," where students work and attend college, sometimes in alternating semesters, sometimes at the same time. This doesn't mean attending college and having a job on or off campus. Rather, co-op programs provide jobs related to your chosen courses or career path and often give you course credit as well as income. Furthermore, students graduating with *relevant* work experience set themselves apart from the annual mass of new college graduates looking for a job each June. For a free brochure, write to the National Commission for Cooperative Education, 360 Huntington Avenue, Boston, MA 02115, or call 617-373-3770.

52

Investment guru Jane Bryant Quinn suggests this college saving plan: As soon as your child is born, invest a set amount each month in stocks for the long term. Once your child turns fourteen, she advises, "take one fourth of the college money out of the market; the next year, take another fourth out, etc., so that all of the money is out of the market when you need it."

This year, almost half of all college students will be twenty-five years or older. If you're faced with tuition hikes, as well as federal and state funding cutbacks, you might try applying for scholarships for "older students" available from: (1) Orville Redenbacher's Second Start Scholarship Program, Box 39101, Chicago, IL 60639; (2) Business & Professional Women's Foundation, 2012 Massachusetts Ave. NW, Washington, D.C. 20036 (202-296-9118); (3) Avon Products Foundation Scholarship Program, 9 West 57th Street, New York, NY 10019 (212-546-6731); and (4) New York Life Foundation Scholarship Program, 51 Madison Avenue, New York, NY 10010 (212-576-7341).

COMPUTERS AND ELECTRONICS

54

Bill, who has a home-based computer business, saves money by printing on both sides of a piece of paper. Sheets with printing on just one side go into a "recycle" box, which he then uses for rough drafts.

55

Buying a computer should be viewed like buying your automobile: Because of the wear and tear on its parts, as well as technology that continues to advance after your purchase, it is a depreciating asset from day one of your ownership. However, you will get the most value from your computer, and postpone its obsolescence, if you view your purchase as investment spending. Buy the largest hard disc drive and most capable chip that you can afford, because the new software that comes to market will be gobbling up all that speed and memory.

56

When you buy a computer, you'll save money if you build yourself a package deal and buy everything at once from one dealer. Additional advantages: Your system will be completely installed (you won't need to hire a computer guru to do it for you) so that all the parts "talk" to each other, and you'll probably get several software packages thrown in.

57

If you buy software by mail order, it will cost less. Check the ads in the computer specialty magazines. However, buy well-known software, unless you like fiddling with problems.

58

Consumer groups repeatedly tell us that extended warranties are rip-offs, but Hewlett-Packard has designed a service for its products that's different. Purchased in box form, much like software, and packaged with the HPLaserJet, DeskJet, ScanJet, and fax products, the HP SupportPack costs 10–15 percent of the purchase price. The package buys three extra years of warranty coverage and includes toll-free phone support and free overnight product replacement. If you have a problem with your product and need replacement just once, you've earned back your investment.

Save money, not to mention time and aggravation, by properly storing your used and unused floppy discs. Keep them away from heat, magnetic fields, and dust.

60

Should you buy *used* electronic equipment for your home office? Yes, if you're shopping for hardware. Computers generally last ten years, and much secondhand equipment is still good. Prices for used goods average thirty percent lower than the best price for new. But don't buy any equipment unless you can test it yourself, with the software you actually use.

61

Some experts argue that most people don't need the fastest and smartest computer available, the 486 (actually, there are more powerful models, but they're still *very* expensive). However, because the 486 outperforms its predecessor, the less powerful but more-than-adequate 386s can be had at bargain-basement prices. Whether you shop retail or mail vendor, ask several salespersons how much power you need for the work your computer has to do.

62

Almost everyone has had the experience of coming into their office or home and finding all their digital clocks flashing. A lot of appliances, including computers, are very sensitive to changes in electrical voltage. Digital clocks and VCRs can be reset very easily, but losing material from your computer memory can be very costly. Protect against such losses by plugging your computer into a "surge protector," available at electronics stores for approximately $50.

63

There is a life cycle in electronics products (also in computer hardware). Newly developed gadgets are often large and very expensive. Then the manufacturers make improvements, building them smaller and cheaper. In its final stage, a product can be so cheap it often falls apart! To get the best value for your money, you'll want to buy a product that is relatively problem-free. To achieve that end, experts recommend that you wait at least a year after the product is introduced before buying.

64

Gadget gurus tell us that extended warranties for appliances, cars, etc., are a waste of money. (You may, however, want peace of mind, and you can't put a price on that.) Another way to look at it is to take the total cost of the extended plan, divide it by the number of years of coverage, and then put that much annually into an interest-earning account. In the first case, you're giving money away; in the second, you're keeping your money and adding to it.

65

If you have small children and you don't want the expense of replacing or repairing your video cassette recorder, buy a VCR lock. It renders your machine impossible to invade.

66

Make cassette tapes for your car from your compact discs (CDs). As long as these are for your *personal* use, you're not violating any copyright laws.

CREDIT CARDS

67

Years ago your only considerations in choosing a credit card company were the annual fee and the interest rate on your finance charges. Now, as more and more nonbank companies offer cards, careful shoppers can get much more. For example, with the GE Rewards card, you receive savings coupons worth $1,000 annually, plus 2 percent back in rewards checks for purchases you make using the card; the coupons may be used toward buying products and services available from twenty-seven participating companies (800-437-3927).

68

Do you have large telephone bills? With the GTE MasterCard, 10 percent of the value of the calls you make on GTE's telephone system is returned to you, up to $50 a year (800-247-2566).

69

If you buy a new car every five years and prefer the Ford models, get yourself the Ford Citibank credit card, one of the new so-called corporate cards (800-374-7777). Over five years, you can accumulate up to $3,500 in credits toward the purchase of a Ford car.

70

Traditional credit cards charge the user an annual fee, but several of the new corporate cards are different. Take, for example, AT&T's Universal card. Your annual fee is waived for life if you transfer balances of $1,000 or more from other cards (800-662-7759). However, be certain you're not incurring higher interest charges.

The credit card business has become so competitive that banks will often drop their fees to keep your business if you threaten to leave for a no-fee card. Furthermore, you can get the annual fee on your credit card reduced or eliminated if you have a good credit history.

One family I know was lured into an electronics store to look at a $2,000–$3,000 home theater system by promises of "Pay nothing for ninety days." On further questioning, however, they learned that the interest rate to finance their purchase was a whopping 18½ percent. The family elected to *save* (and *keep* the interest) for their wide-screen TV and buy later on.

With the GM Card, one of the newest corporate credit cards, users can accumulate $3,500, over seven years' time, in credits toward the purchase of a GM car. You also accumulate credits when you use the card at specific companies when you rent a car, make long distance phone calls, stay at hotels, and buy gasoline and other products (800-846-2273).

If you travel frequently by airplane for business, chances are you've already enrolled in one or more of the many "frequent flyer" programs offered by most major airline companies. These programs allow you to earn mileage credit toward future travel. However, credit cards have gotten into the flying act, too. For example, Citibank's AAdvantage MasterCard or Visa card gives you a mile on American Airlines for every dollar you spend on purchases (800-359-4444).

More than two hundred charities raise money by putting their names on a Visa or MasterCard. Depending on the deal they strike with the issuing bank, the charity gets a small percentage of your purchases. As everyone knows, charitable donations are tax deductible, but cuts from credit card purchases are not. You'll save money if you shop for the lowest rate card and give directly to the charity of your choice.

You can send for a list of low-fee, low-rate credit cards by sending $5 to RAM Research, P.O. Box 1700, Frederick, MD 21702 (301-695-4660). In addition, *Money* magazine, available by subscription, at newsstands, and at your local library, has a column on "THE BEST CREDIT CARDS IN THE U.S." for those who carry a monthly balance, as well as for those who pay each month in full.

Do you want to qualify for a low-rate credit card? If you've just changed your job or address, wait twelve months before applying. And check your credit reports to be sure all your accounts are reported accurately. Look for credit reporting agencies, such as TRW, Trans Union, and CBI/Equifax in the Yellow Pages.

DIVORCE

78

It is estimated that, on average, mediated divorces cost any-
where from one tenth to one half what contested divorces do.
However, you should *not* use a divorce mediator if you doubt
your spouse's financial honesty, if he is involved in criminal
activity, if one of you is mentally incompetent, or if there is
current physical abuse.

79

When choosing your divorce attorney, narrow your search to
three candidates. Then take the time to interview each one.
This is worth the expense, but be sure to ask about the consultation fee before the interview.

Many divorce attorneys will ask for a retainer fee up front. Make sure your retainer agreement spells out which expenses you'll be expected to pay and who will do the work.

Your divorce attorney will bill you for each time you talk with her or him on the phone or in person. To keep conversations focused, and costs down, my friend Sharon always wrote out her questions before talking to her attorney and took notes at every meeting.

Because alimony is taxable and child support is not, a woman might assume she should try to negotiate as much child support as possible. Not necessarily. What you're looking for is the greatest after-tax income possible. If the husband is heavily taxed, his burden will be lessened if he pays hefty alimony, which he can deduct. If he earns a lot more than the wife, his payments can include some of the taxes she will owe.

The timing of a couple's divorce is important. It is usually prudent to have it occur at the beginning of the year so you can file your previous year's taxes using the cheaper rates for married people. Once you are divorced, you can no longer file a joint return.

Legal fees for a divorce cannot be deducted from your income tax. However, you can deduct any fees you pay for tax advice. Ask your lawyer for an itemized bill showing how much you spent for tax help. Furthermore, you may write off any costs associated with securing or collecting support payments.

Did you know that divorced women can collect on their ex-husbands' Social Security if the marriage lasted at least ten years? You can file for benefits at age sixty-two, even if your ex-husband hasn't retired, provided you've been divorced two years or more.

FINANCIAL PLANNING

86

"Procrastination is the number one enemy of investing money," says financial planner Chris Beale. "People are stalled by insecurity about their knowledge and by uncertainty about where the market is going. However, while fear keeps them from acting, it also causes them to lose purchasing power due to inflation and taxes. *Do it*," he says. "Just do it."

87

You have two risks where choosing investments is concerned: first, you risk the possibility that you'll lose your principal. But there's a second, and potentially much larger, risk that most people forget: Unless you invest at a rate of return greater than the inflation rate, you'll lose purchasing power; that is, your dollar today won't buy a dollar's worth of tomorrow's goods and services. For example, at today's low CD (certificate of deposit) rates and with inflation as low as 4 percent, you will halve your purchasing power in eighteen years.

To make informed investment decisions, everyone should understand the "seventy-two rule": Seventy-two divided by an investment product's yield equals the number of years it will take to double your money, (assuming the income is reinvested). For example, if you buy municipal bonds yielding 8 percent, seventy-two divided by eight equals nine years to double your investment.

If you seek the services of a financial planner, it's essential that you understand how they charge. Most planners earn their living by charging you (1) a commission on the investment products you buy, (2) an hourly fee for their advice, or (3) a combination of the two. Ask the planner to disclose in advance the fees or commissions you'll pay on each transaction. In addition, ask to see his or her ADV, the registration form filed with the Securities and Exchange Commission, which discloses how the planner does business. Finally, you can ask if the planner is a member of the International Association of Financial Planners. Members of IAFP are concerned with industry standards and with staying up on their own continuing education.

Stockbrokers and insurance agents who call themselves "financial consultants" are not the same as financial planners. The latter designation is awarded to individuals who earn their Certified Financial Planner title from the College for Financial Planning in Denver, Colorado. To receive the CFP designation, one must complete a series of six courses and a comprehensive exam, as well as field experience.

The International Association for Financial Planning (IAFP) has a toll-free number (800-945-IAFP) if you would like free information about financial planning and a list of five financial planners. They will also send you a sample disclosure form if you want to review a planner's professional qualifications and methods of compensation before entering into a business relationship.

One question I've always found helpful in interviewing financial planners is, "How much annual revenue do you look for from a good client?" In other words, how much activity makes a client worthwhile to a planner? This is one way I determine if I'll be worth their time. If I don't meet their minimum, I continue to look for one who believes that "from little acorns big oaks grow."

According to Louis Rukeyser, syndicated columnist and the host of *Wall Street Week* on PBS, "The reckless may occasionally crash on life's shoals, to be sure, but those who seek to eliminate all risk are guaranteed to remain there forever. There is a tremendous risk in doing nothing."

There are two forces that affect your ability to accumulate assets: rate of return and time. "Be patient," advises Milt, a portfolio manager. "Young people have plenty of time because they're young. Even a sixty-five-year-old has an average of another twenty years to live. And almost every investment is cyclical. What's low in price now will come up; conversely, what's up now will fall."

You've heard the old adage, "Don't put all your eggs in one basket." It applies especially to investing. "You have to diversify," says Jeanne, a top-selling broker. "Spread your dollars across several types of investments, as well as across different industries. This strategy protects you in case the price of one company's stock drops dramatically."

If you have highly appreciated assets, such as stocks or real estate, and would like to sell some, but the reality of capital gains taxes is stopping you, a charitable remainder trust (CRT) is one solution. The CRT sells the assets, avoiding capital gains tax, and reinvests them to produce income for you and your family members (or some other noncharitable beneficiary). You also get a partial tax deduction for your contribution. At the end of your lifetime, or after a specified period of up to twenty years, what remains in the trust will go to a qualified charity of your choice. A CRT is an increasingly popular way to reduce estate taxes.

INSURANCE

97

Insurance-rate services, long available to agents, are now making their data bases available to consumers. Quotesmith Corporation (800-556-9393), for example, will provide you with a ranking of twenty-five to fifty policies—term life, individual health, Medicare supplement, long-term care, etc.—according to the criteria you specify. The cost is $15.

98

If you have to stop working because of a disabling illness or accident, tell your insurance agent. You may be able to stop paying premiums on your life, health, and disability insurance while still keeping the coverage.

99

If your insurance company refuses a claim you think it should pay, complain to your state insurance department. A good insurance commissioner may be able to help you collect.

100

When you get a new-car loan, a mortgage, or a credit card, you may be offered "credit insurance" that will pay your outstanding debt on the loan in case of death, disability, or unemployment. According to the National Insurance Consumers Organization (NICO), credit insurance rates, which vary by state, are far too high, and the companies take in much more than they pay out. The same goes for mortgage protection insurance. If you have good life insurance and disability coverage, you shouldn't need anything more to cover your bills in an emergency.

AUTOMOBILE INSURANCE

101

You should keep insurance costs in mind when you buy a car. Choose from models that cost less to insure. Your insurance company can provide you with this information.

102

If you drive fewer than 7,500 miles per year, it usually means lower car insurance rates.

103

In addition to the familiar strategy of raising your deductible to lower your automobile insurance premium, you should cancel collision coverage on older cars, or when the collision premium equals 10 percent or more of the car's market value.

104

Some insurance companies allow you to cancel collision coverage on your automobile while you're on a long vacation and leave your garaged car behind.

105

Many automobile insurance companies will lower your premiums if you choose a lawsuit limitation where you agree *not* to sue another motorist for nonmedical costs, or "pain and suffering." Also car insurance costs less if you keep your teenagers or adult children who live with you on your policy, rather than on a separate policy. Similarly, one policy covering more than one car should cost you less than a policy for each car.

106

In twenty-nine states and Washington, D.C., adults who have completed a defensive-driving course may be entitled to a discount on their car insurance.

107

Very often, insurance premiums are lower if both your automobile and homeowners' policy are with the same company.

108

According to Evelyn, an insurance agent, "The most effective force in keeping down car insurance premium costs is a good driving record."

109

Special features such as automatic safety belts, air bags, and antilock brakes, which may add to the purchase price of your car, may also pay for themselves over time in the form of discounts on your insurance premiums.

110

You may be entitled to a discount on your car insurance if you show proof of purchase for approved antitheft devices.

111

Most parents shudder when they contemplate car insurance premiums for a teenage new driver. However, you may receive a discount if your new driver has completed student driver training, if he or she gets good grades in high school or college, or if your student lives more than one hundred miles from the family home.

$$\boxed{112}$$

Ralph Nader, America's tireless consumer advocate, does not recommend rental-car insurance. "The cost of it is too expensive," he says. "The $500 deductible coverage is typically $5 a day, or $1,825 a year. You'd have to average three and a half accidents a year to break even." Your own liability or car insurance most likely covers you, and all three major credit card issuers offer automatic free coverage when you charge a rental car to their gold or business cards. Credit card coverage is usually supplemental insurance, however; if you bang up the car, you will be expected to turn first to your own insurance policy.

$$\boxed{113}$$

You may need a special endorsement to your auto insurance to cover a cellular phone that is permanently installed in your car. A portable cellular phone should be covered by your *homeowners'* insurance.

DISABILITY INSURANCE

$$\boxed{114}$$

"Most people buy insurance to protect their valuable assets against loss, but many never insure their most important resource: their ability to work and earn income," says Alan Weiss, a Connecticut financial planner. The best policy, according to Alan, is one that pays benefits when the insured is unable to perform his or her occupation. Other key features to look for include: a non-cancelable policy, a guaranteed renewable policy, a cost-of-living increase, a waiver of premium, and the right to purchase additional insurance as your income rises.

HOMEOWNERS' INSURANCE

115

I learned a valuable insurance lesson the hard way: It's easy to be roped in by a new company promising lower homeowners' insurance premiums, but make sure they will insure you *before* you change companies. I switched companies, completed endless forms, interrupted my work to be at home for inspections, and made my first payment. Afterward, I was notified that they were canceling my policies because of some minute detail of my home's construction. Thankfully, my old company welcomed me back, but my hasty switch didn't save me a dime—indeed, it cost me money.

116

It pays to examine your homeowners' insurance policy carefully. Coverage usually comes in three types: HO-1, HO-2, and HO-3. HO-1 is the most basic and the cheapest, but it doesn't cover water damage from pipes. Costs vary widely, but even HO-3 should cost only 10–20 percent more than HO-1 coverage.

117

If you retired this year, or turned fifty, you may qualify for a discount on your homeowners' insurance policy. The same goes for your automobile coverage.

118

Most homeowners' policies cover you for loss or theft of items whose individual value does not exceed $1,000. If you bought a computer, jewelry, furs, or expensive home electronics and you want to insure them for their full value, be certain to add a rider to your policy.

119

Starting a home-based business is another reason to closely examine your homeowners' coverage. Make sure you protect your business equipment and have enough liability insurance.

120

If rapidly changing real estate values have driven your home's replacement cost up, or down, it's time to reexamine your homeowners' insurance policy. If home prices are substantially lower, your premium may also go down.

121

Did you make major home improvements this year? If so, you should adjust your replacement cost on your homeowners' insurance. Your premium will probably go up, but the alternative is to suffer a major loss and come up short on your claim.

122

If you install safety systems such as burglar alarms, sprinklers, dead-bolt locks, or smoke detectors, you can earn discounts of 2–20 percent off your homeowners' insurance premium.

123

Robberies are expensive, not to mention nerve-racking. Rather than installing an elaborate and expensive home-security system, you can reduce your risk of a break-in while you are away by using low-cost light timers and by taking other steps to give the appearance that your home is occupied. Arrange to have the grass mowed and the mail and daily paper stopped, and ask a neighbor to watch for packages that might arrive during your absence.

LIFE INSURANCE

124

Throughout the many arguments, pro and con, about life insurance, there is one immutable fact: Life insurance is the only use of money that pays the beneficiary when someone dies, and that payment is not taxable income. In the words of one insured: "Life insurance may not make for the best investment, but investments make for even worse insurance." (Note: Even though the payout is income tax-free to the beneficiary, unless that recipient is your spouse, the money is usually included in your estate and is taxed when you die.)

125

Wait until an agent has recommended a life insurance policy and then ask if there is a lower-commission version. At least twenty-five companies now offer cheaper versions of their standard term or universal life policies. Agents aren't likely to volunteer this information, except to consumers who know about the discounts.

126

Ask about life insurance discounts. Most companies will lower premiums for non-smokers and some will do so for people who do regular aerobic exercise.

127

Here's a way to keep the proceeds of your life insurance policy out of your estate: Create an irrevocable life insurance trust that owns the policy on your life. Then, when you die, the trust receives the proceeds and, according to your wishes, pays income to your spouse for life and then passes the principal directly to your children. There are many angles and restrictions, however, which you should discuss with your attorney.

128

Margaret, who has a good relationship with her two adult children, chose a simpler way to keep life insurance proceeds out of her estate: Her children bought a policy on her life, but she gives them the yearly premium amounts to pay costs. As long as Margaret doesn't own the policy, the proceeds aren't part of her taxable estate.

129

You can save money if you order life insurance by mail, because you will not be paying for an agent's commission. To investigate some of the better mail-order companies, contact the National Insurance Consumer Organization (NICO) in Alexandria, Virginia (703-549-8050).

130

According to the National Insurance Consumer Organization (NICO), annually renewable term insurance provides the most coverage for the least cost. Furthermore, if you take the difference in cost between a term policy and a more expensive cash-value policy and *invest* that difference, you'll earn more money on your own than a cash-value policy will accrue. For a free list of several low-cost term insurance policies, call SelectQuote (800-343-1985).

131

There are more than two thousand U.S. insurance companies that sell life insurance. If you're interested in *term* life insurance—the kind where you pay a premium for a certain amount of time and there's no accrual of cash value—get some help sifting through the many choices by calling Insurance Information, Inc., at 800-472-5800. For a modest fee, they will send you a report on up to five of the lowest-cost companies to fill your needs.

132

With low-load life insurance, consumers buy directly from the company, as opposed to buying from an insurance agent or through fee-for-service advisors. With traditional, agent-bought life insurance, much or all of your first year's premium goes to your agent. A low-load policy, on the other hand, puts most of that policy to work for you right away. There are numerous books available that explain how to buy insurance on your own, and you can contact the National Insurance Consumer Organization (NICO) in Alexandria, Virginia (703-549-8050).

133

My friend Roger, an insurance agent, cautions consumers against being drawn to a life insurance policy simply because it has a low premium. "Often the lowest premium policies are not 'guaranteed renewable,' " he says. "Many low-cost policies require an annual physical, and if you develop a problem, the company may cancel your coverage."

134

A big advantage of a cash-value life insurance policy is that you can borrow against the amount accrued. However, if you don't expect to do so, look for a life insurance company that provides "direct recognition," that is, higher interest or dividends to policyholders who don't borrow.

135

The National Consumer Insurance Organization (NICO) can tell you what cash-value life insurance policies are actually earning. To check out a proposed new policy, send NICO the policy illustration that the agent gives you. To check your current policy, send the in-force ledger statement. NICO charges for these services, but the fees are small and well worth the cost if you can avoid making a bad purchase. For evaluation instructions, call NICO in Alexandria, Virginia (703-549-8050).

136

Cash-value life insurance is tax-deferred until you begin to draw on it. Keep in mind that you'll be taxed on the difference between the cash value and the total premiums you've paid.

137

A benefit to the cash-value variety of life insurance is that it's considered a "hidden asset" and *not* taken into consideration when you're applying for financial aid, government or private, to send your child to college. The same is true for annuities and other tax-deferred retirement plans.

138

Since some life insurance companies got into trouble earlier in this decade, the most important question you need to ask of your policy, especially if you bought it after 1980, is *Will it last for life?* Ask your life insurance agent to get you an "in-force ledger statement" stating how long your cash-value policy will stay in force if you continue paying the same premiums. It should pay the full amount, no matter how long the insured person lives. Because interest rates have declined, you may have to increase your premiums to prevent your policy from lapsing before you die.

139

A friend of mine bought an annuity (a contract with an insurance company that invests your funds and returns them to you in one of several ways that you choose) and expected to receive a fixed income for life, but his company collapsed and began paying annuitants fifty cents on the dollar. To guard against the demise of your annuity company, experts recommend that you divide your money among two or three insurers with top safety ratings.

140

If you have a two-income family, do you need two life insurance policies? Some say you do, but who can cram two premiums into an already tight budget? A growing number of insurance companies are promoting a new product, "first-to-die joint life," a cash-value policy that insures two persons and pays the benefit at the time of the first death. Premiums are typically 25 percent less than for two separate cash-value policies. (However, you build less cash value than you would with two policies.)

141

Does an annuity make sense for *you*? If you are already making the maximum contribution of pretax dollars to an IRA, 401 (k), or other similar retirement plan, and you can afford to set aside even more money until age fifty-nine and a half, then you should look at tax-deferred annuities. Your research should compare the advantages of the annuity versus a low-cost, no-load mutual fund (even without the tax benefits).

142

After you retire, does it make sense to keep your cash-value life insurance? Investment counselors argue that you can probably get a better return by investing the cash value, but few retired people want the responsibility of making investment decisions. One way to turn your cash value into income is to convert your policy into an annuity.

INTERIOR DECORATING

143

If you want to save money *and* time on redecorating when you're raising kids, use washable wallpapers and semigloss paints, which are easier to keep clean.

144

Carol, an interior decorator, is frequently called in to help a client *after* costly mistakes have been made. "You must start with a decorating plan for each room, including color scheme, floor plan, and window treatments," she says. "Shop around for a professional decorator who can assist you in making the right choices. If you simply need advice, and will do your own shopping, you might pay a design fee or an hourly rate. On the other hand, if your decorator will provide your furnishings, you will pay a markup over the cost of your purchases."

145

Quantity of fabric makes or breaks draperies, according to my friend Marlene, a do-it-yourself decorator. "When you're on a budget, use less expensive fabric, but use a lot of it for proper fullness—at least double the width of the window—rather than skimping with a more expensive fabric."

146

Small, round end tables with table skirts and overdrapes are much less expensive than antique or even reproduction tables. The fabric will also add color and interest to the room.

147

If you can't afford a new dining room set, choose the low-cost alternative that interior decorator Helen suggests: "Cover a forty-eight-inch round commercial conference table with a pretty table skirt for your dining table. This will seat six comfortably."

148

"When you can't afford to fill a room with furniture right away, start with one seating grouping in the center," advises Gerry, a decorator with a department store chain. "Light it well and fill the empty areas of the room with floor plants. As your budget allows, expand your furniture outward. This strategy will avoid a haphazard look until the room can be finished."

INVESTMENT OPTIONS

149

Keeping track of your investment portfolio requires lots of time. Why not share the work and join an investment club? According to the National Association of Investors Corporation, the average club account is nearly nine years old and has earned 14.9 percent annually over that period, compared with 12.3 percent for the S&P 500. For instructions on how to start a club, write to NAIC, P.O. Box 220, Royal Oak, MI 48067, (313-543-0612).

150

If you have a liquid emergency fund that's enough to cover three months' living expenses, don't automatically keep feeding money into that savings or money-market account. Look for more aggressive investments likely to return bigger rewards over the long term.

BONDS

151

If you have at least $5,000 to invest, you can earn even more interest than money market mutual funds are paying by buying an individual bond that has a fixed maturity date. Be sure to select a high-quality bond, with a high rating from more than one bond-rating service, which you purchase through a broker or some banks.

152

The day of the month you buy a bond and the day you redeem it can affect your yield. According to my friend Jack, a bond expert, "Since the issue date of a bond is recorded as the month and year of the purchase, you should buy at the end of the month and sell at the beginning. You receive interest for the entire month regardless of what day the transaction takes place."

153

Zero coupon bonds, bought and sold through brokers, are so-called because you buy them at a discount and redeem them at face value when they mature. One drawback: You must pay tax each year on a portion of the "original issue discount," the difference between the issue price and the face value at maturity. However, you won't actually receive the interest until the bond matures, or you sell it. Therefore, taxable zero coupon bonds are often recommended for retirement plan funds, where taxes are deferred until you retire and the bonds have matured.

154

Money you don't give the government is money in your pocket. Tax-free municipal bonds are a sound investment, especially when you buy municipals that are rated "AAA" by bond-rating agencies. For example, a 5.8 percent tax-free yield equals a taxable equivalent yield of 8.75 percent in a 31 percent federal tax bracket and a 9.45 percent yield in a 36 percent tax bracket.

155

Before you jump into the municipal bond arena, make sure you look at the whole picture: (1) Most states tax the interest on municipals issued out of state, and Illinois is one that taxes most in-state bonds as well; (2) Municipals are tax free for ordinary tax, but are subject to "alternative minimum tax"; and (3) If you are in a low tax bracket, your net investment return from municipals may not be worthwhile. Check with your accountant.

156

It used to be you couldn't purchase municipal bonds for less than $5,000, but now some cities, a handful of schools and public colleges, and a few water and sewer districts are selling "minibonds" for as low as $500 and priced at a discount from face value. Definitely a "buy-and-hold" investment, they aren't callable, but there is no secondary market, either. A Denver minibond bought in 1993 for $500 delivers $1,000 in 2004, a yield to maturity of six percent.

157

There are many ways to own in-state municipal bonds: bond mutual funds, an in-state unit trust (a portfolio of ten to fifteen bonds), and individual bonds. If you intend to reinvest your income, choose a bond *fund*, which allows you to write checks. If you prefer predictable monthly or quarterly dividends, use a trust.

158

Individual bonds avoid the costs of funds and trusts, but unless you invest $50,000 to $100,000 in five to ten bonds, broker commissions may eat into their yield advantage.

159

Series EE United States savings bonds now offer several important advantages: They are not subject to state and local taxes, and if you bought them after January 1, 1990, and use them for college tuition (held in *your* name, not your child's), they're completely tax-free when you cash them in. (However, as with most tax breaks these days, the exclusion is phased out for middle- and upper-income taxpayers.)

160

If you hold series EE bonds longer than six months, the interest rate increases for each half-year you hold them, up to five years. After that period, the interest rate "floats," with a new rate published every six months. (For current rate information, call 800-487-2663.)

161

You can own a savings bond for as little as $25, paying no commissions or transaction fee. These also force you to save, because you don't receive the interest payments until you redeem the bond.

162

It doesn't pay to hold series EE savings bonds forever because after forty years they stop paying interest. If you have some that were issued in the late 1940s or early 1950s, cash them in and invest the money where it can do some good.

163

Interest on series EE savings bonds is credited only twice a year. To receive the maximum interest, you should redeem your bonds in the same month you bought them or on the six-month anniversary.

164

Longer-term bonds generally have higher yields than their short-term counterparts. By building a "laddered" portfolio, you can insure that your fixed-income investments earn higher interest, even in periods of falling interest rates. A typical strategy is to invest the same amount of money in ten bonds, one of them maturing in each of ten consecutive years. Each year when one tenth of your portfolio matures, you buy another ten-year bond. After a few years, you will have 10 ten-year bonds, paying a higher yield, with one bond maturing every year.

165

In her popular book *Your Wealth-Building Years: Financial Planning for 18- to 38-year-olds*, Adriane Berg writes about the tax-saving strategy known as "bondswapping." If you own bonds that have decreased in value, you should sell them at a loss before the end of the year. Use the money to buy new bonds that pay the same amount of income. As long as the maturity dates are longer than the bonds you sold, you'll be able to buy the same face value of bonds and receive the same income.

166

Because the interest on U.S. Treasury securities (bills, notes, and bonds) is not subject to state or local income taxes, they may earn more for you than CDs (certificates of deposit) after tax. The minimum investment for one-year Treasuries is $10,000, but you can invest for longer terms for $5,000 and $1,000. Treasuries are available from your broker.

MUTUAL FUNDS

167

The trouble with "riskless" investments—savings accounts and short-term certificates of deposit—is that they're barely keeping up with inflation, which means you're losing money after taxes. Even conservative investors should consider moving some savings to top-paying money-market mutual funds, tax-free bond funds, or mutual funds that invest in dividend-paying stocks.

168

There are many mutual funds today—stock funds, bond funds, balanced funds, etc.—that offer the option of buying shares with a fixed amount of money that is transferred electronically from your account at a specified time (once a month, quarterly, etc.). Some funds require an investment of $2,000 or more, but when you invest automatically, some accept as little as $50 or $100 a month. This is one way small investors can increase their assets. The prospectus for the fund will identify this feature.

169

Money-market mutual funds often feature check writing as an added benefit. Beware: Each time you write a check on the mutual fund, you have *sold* a portion of your investment. You must allocate a portion of your investment cost, or basis, to each check written and report a capital gain or loss on your income tax return. This can create headaches for whoever prepares your tax return and also lead to some unpleasant surprises on April 15!

170

If you have less than $5,000, you can own higher-yielding bonds by buying shares of bond mutual funds. The short-term bond funds, which invest in bonds maturing in four years or less, are the least risky. And you can grow your investment by electing to have your dividends reinvested in more shares. Recent bond fund yields have been 2.5 percent above one-year CDs.

171

In shopping for mutual funds that will pay off, look at the "no-load" varieties. Your only charge is the annual management fee, which should be no more than 1 percent. There are no sales fees when you buy or sell, and no marketing, or 12b-1, fees are taken out each year. Furthermore, as of a July 7, 1993, ruling, no-loads can't deplete fund assets by more than 0.25 percent a year for sales and marketing costs. You buy these funds directly from the company by calling their toll-free number. For a directory of mutual funds that charge no sales fees, send $3 to 100% No-Load Mutual Fund Council, 1501 Broadway, Suite 1809 New York, NY 10036 (212-768-2477).

172

The advantage most frequently cited for mutual funds is that they permit a small investor to diversify among a number of investments; that is, the fund invests in many stocks, bonds, Treasuries, or combinations of these. Also, by owning shares in more than one fund, an individual can diversify even more. Some advisors recommend that you buy shares in one family of funds (like Fidelity or Vanguard), which allows the investor to move in and out of funds without incurring a sales charge. (Remember, however, that each time you move out of a fund, you trigger a sale and resulting capital gain or loss. This is true even if you immediately reinvest in another fund.)

173

Certain discount brokers are now making it possible for you to own top no-load funds from a variety of families in and out of a single, consolidated account. For no more than it costs to deal with each fund family separately, investors can assemble portfolios of funds from a wide variety of sponsors with one phone call and can track all their holdings in a single monthly account statement.

174

Every accountant, financial planner, tax attorney, or expert you can name will tell you that you'll hold onto more of the money you make if you keep good records of it. With mutual funds, the key is to track the "cost basis" (which includes income reinvested), of your shares—the amount you'll compare with the selling price to figure your taxable gain or tax-saving loss. Keep notices of each transaction until it shows up on a cumulative quarterly or annual statement. Then you can discard the old statements. Just make sure you have a written record of every purchase and redemption.

175

"Index funds" are mutual funds that attempt to mirror the composition of a specified stock or bond market index, such as the Standard & Poor's 500. Their fees are lower, and they often outperform other funds. (There are no stocks to analyze, no stock pickers to pay, and few stocks are traded. Thus, a typical expense ratio is 0.2 percent a year versus an average of 1.5 percent for all stock mutual funds.) According to Morningstar Mutual Fund Service, 514 U.S. diversified equity mutual funds had an average annualized total return of 14.65 percent for the ten years prior to September 30, 1992. The equivalent annual return for the Standard & Poor's 500 Index during the same period was 17.5 percent.

176

"Closed-end" mutual funds trade just like common stock, with standard broker commissions. Shares may trade at, above, or below a fund's Net Asset Value (NAV). As a buyer, you want to purchase a closed-end fund's shares at a discount; that is, at less than its NAV.

177

In choosing to invest in one of the new do-it-for-me "asset allocation" funds, where managers divide up your investment pot for you between stocks, bonds and money market instruments, there are three key factors to keep in mind: 1) Have a clear understanding of the goals and strategy of the fund manager; 2) Keep track of changes in goals and strategies; and 3) Don't use asset allocation as an excuse to forget about your investment.

178

"Asset management accounts" (AMAs), first introduced fifteen years ago by Merrill Lynch and now offered by every major U.S. broker, combine the features of checking, money-market, and broker accounts, with the convenience of one monthly statement, plus a variety of additional perks. However, some AMA detractors maintain these accounts are more attractive for brokers than investors. If you keep a lot of cash on hand, you'll want to look for the highest yield of the money funds. Ask also about annual fees, the minimum required to open an account, and how often idle cash is "swept" into the money funds.

STOCKS

179

The arguments for investing in common stocks over the long term are in the numbers: The average return over sixty-seven years for short-term Treasury bills has been 3.7 percent, so with 3.1 percent inflation over that same period, you're treading water. The return on long-term thirty-year bonds has been 4.8 percent, while the return on U.S. common stocks has been 11.1 percent.

180

Instead of stretching for 20 percent–plus returns on risky stocks, you should aim instead for average annual profits of 8–9 percent on safer choices. A recent survey found that experts think shares of large U.S. companies will return an average of 8.8 percent annually over the next five years, with 3.6

percent inflation. So after inflation, you would earn 5.2 percent a year. That's a third below the 8 percent real return stocks have averaged since 1950—but better than a loss.

181

There are many reasons to buy a particular stock—a low price-to-earnings (P/E) ratio, a low price compared to the fifty-two week high, an important product in an emerging industry, and so on—but *Money* magazine and others suggest you can beat the market with stocks heavily owned by insiders. Public companies that are closely held by one family often don't pay dividends that are taxable. Instead, they put excess cash into new products and plants that sustain growth—and tax-deferred appreciation of stock prices. A new question to ask your broker: How much of the stock is held by insiders?

182

As an alternative to bank certificates of deposit (CDs), buy utility company stocks. They're relatively safe and pay hefty dividends, which make them ideal for retirees and others who need a steady flow of income. Note: Historically, power companies have generally paid higher dividends than many natural-gas and telephone firms. Look for electric utilities whose dividend payouts are less than 75 percent of earnings, leaving room for a hefty dividend hike.

183

There are more than nine hundred companies that allow investors to increase their shares without brokers by using automatic dividend reinvestment. But corporations such as Exxon, Texaco, Mobil, W. R. Grace, Johnson Controls, and Procter & Gamble have set up a way for investors to make their first purchase. For a booklet listing companies offering such plans, write to Evergreen Enterprises, P.O. Box 763, Laurel, MD 20725 (301-953-1861).

184

Whatever you do, buy and hold stocks over a long period. The twentieth century has seen fifty stock market declines of 10 percent or more, and fifteen of these have exceeded twenty-five percent. However, over the long haul, stocks have been the most successful place for individuals to invest.

185

Do you agonize over the perfect time to buy and sell shares of stock or mutual funds? Take the emotion out of the decision and use the systematic approach to investing known as "dollar cost averaging." This means an investor puts a certain sum of money in the same investment at regular intervals, for example: $500 worth of stock on the first day of the month for twelve months. By using a set amount, you will purchase more shares when prices are lower and fewer shares when prices are higher.

186

There are many reputable brokers in the industry, but if you want to make sure yours is honest from the start, the National Association of Securities Dealers can get you the full disciplinary record of any broker. Call 800-289-9999.

187

People know that the safest stocks or mutual funds are the ones with proven histories of success, but the faint of heart wring their hands and cry, "But how do I find sound companies?" A good broker or financial adviser can provide you with lists of companies whose profits have risen steadily over twenty years, or of companies who have raised their dividends every year for the past twenty-five. These lists show up regularly in the business press. Be a savvy investor. Read often and ask questions.

188

Every investor hopes to buy low and sell high, but what if your timing was wrong and a stock starts to tumble? You can reduce your losses by placing a "stop-loss order" at the time you buy the stock. You might instruct your broker, for example, to sell the stock if its price goes down 20 percent. (Note: This is a strong argument for having a full-service broker, because few discounters accept stop-loss orders.)

189

Numerous studies support the theory that you will have greater investment returns if you buy stocks with low price-to-earnings (P/E) ratios. One study, which adjusted its portfolio every quarter to contain stocks with P/Es under ten, produced a return over nine years of 14 percent.

190

A stock-buying strategy I have sometimes used is to purchase shares of a "blue chip" company that has announced a stock split of, say, two for one. Then I sit back and watch the price of those newly divided shares grow (I hope!). However, you must be a "shareholder of record" before a certain date in order to benefit from the split. Several business days elapse before your buy is made known to the stock company. If you want to take advantage of a stock split, confirm the timing with your broker.

191

If the 1980s was the decade of free spending, the 1990s finds consumers cutting back. If you would like to invest in the growing trend to spend less, consider the following companies suggested by *Kiplinger's Personal Finance Magazine*: AutoZone (do-it-yourself auto parts and supplies), Consolidated Stores (close-out stores), and Dayton Hudson (whose discount subsidiary is Target stores) traded on the New York Stock Exchange; and Fred's (discount retail), F&M Distributors (discount drug stores), and Cott (private-label soft drinks) traded on the over-the-counter (OTC) exchange.

TAX-DEFERRED INVESTMENTS

192

You'll save money if you set up an Individual Retirement Account (IRA) because your earnings accumulate tax-free until they are withdrawn (after age fifty-nine and a half). And here's a good way to make sure you comply: Instead of waiting till the end of the year and then scrambling around to find $2,000 (the maximum that you're allowed to contribute annually), invest a little each month or pay period.

193

If you can manage to contribute $2,000 to a money-market mutual fund IRA at the *beginning* of the year, and then each month have one-twelfth (or $166.67) transferred into a stock mutual fund, you would have the benefit of dollar-cost averaging, and your funds would be working for you all year.

194

When was the last time you checked up on your 401(k)? You're doing your job by contributing to it every pay period, and ideally your employer is kicking in also. Get to know your guaranteed investment contract (GIC) because the "guarantee" is only as good as the solvency of the issuing insurer. Ask your employer for the names of the insurance companies whose GICs are used in your plan's fixed-rate account. Then ask for ratings of their claims-paying ability.

195

Make sure your savings in an employer-sponsored plan are adequately diversified. If you're a long way from retirement and your money is piling up in a fixed-income account, you're missing out on the appreciation offered by stock-oriented funds.

196

According to my friend Lori, a credit counselor, the best IRA investment for the unemployed is a safe money-market mutual fund that preserves the principal while giving you ready access to cash.

197

As of December 1993, the Federal Deposit Insurance Corporation (FDIC) will insure your savings up to a total of $100,000 at one bank. If you have several kinds of self-directed retirement plans, such as IRAs or Keoghs, as well as taxable accounts, in the same bank and your total is more than $100,000, a cautious saver will move one or more accounts to another bank.

198

Whenever you move a tax-deferred account, be sure you make it a "trustee-to-trustee" rollover. If a check is written to you and you then deposit it in a new retirement account, the check issuer must withhold 20 percent in federal tax, which you cannot recover until you file your tax return.

LEGAL EXPENSES

199

Giving power of attorney to a spouse, adult child, or friend saves money. Otherwise, if you become ill or incapacitated and are unable to make decisions for yourself, someone has to go to court and appoint a conservator, incurring court costs and attorney's fees.

200

Single persons or people with few assets frequently claim that they don't need a will. However, under the provisions of a will, you can greatly reduce administrative costs after your death by waiving the requirements of your state—perhaps posting a

Legal Expenses

bond, filing an inventory, and petitioning for settlement of the
estate. The cost of preparing a will is much less than the cost
of carrying out these requirements.

201

Have you named a beneficiary on your bank accounts, retirement accounts, and/or Treasury securities? This move does *not*
avoid estate taxes, if your assets are large enough to owe them,
but it does keep the funds out of the time-consuming probate
process. After your death, the beneficiary can get the funds
immediately by showing identification and proof of death.

MEDICAL COSTS

202

What can you do to reduce the cost of your medical care—health insurance premiums, doctors' bills, medicines, etc.? While the government searches for solutions, there are specific things individuals can do to remain healthy and therefore stay out of doctors' offices, pharmacies, and hospitals: Don't smoke, eat a balanced diet, don't drink too much alcohol, and get regular exercise.

203

Insurance watchdogs say you don't need "cancer insurance." These policies cost about $250 a year and pay benefits if you turn out to be the one person out of three who gets cancer during his or her lifetime. However, your comprehensive major medical coverage should insure you against all types of maladies, making a cancer policy redundant.

204

Recent studies have shown that aspirin helps prevent heart disease. Actually, unless you've had a heart attack, atherosclerosis, or unstable angina, all you need is one-fourth of a tablet. Some pharmaceutical companies are introducing quarter-dose aspirin tablets at three times the cost of the full-dose variety. To save money, cut up a 325-milligram tablet yourself, or take a children's aspirin (check with your physician first).

205

It's estimated that buying generic drugs (with your doctor's approval), instead of the brand name variety, over-the-counter or as a prescription, can reduce your medicine costs by 30 percent. Also, if a drug is needed over weeks or months, buying in quantity can reduce the price even further.

206

You can lower your medical costs if you're willing to give up some freedom of choice. One option is to join a health maintenance organization (HMO) where your fees are much lower, but you must agree to go to the group's doctors for all your health care. With HMOs, there are no forms to file, no deductible to pay before coverage begins, fees can be as low as $2 per office visit, and all preventive care is covered. Some forms of "managed care," called open-ended HMOs, allow you to go outside the doctor group if you're willing to pay more.

207

You can save up to 40 percent of medical costs by setting up a "medical reimbursement account" with your employer. The savings to you come from the fact that the money is set aside before any of your taxes are deducted. Decide at the beginning of the year how much you think you're going to pay for medical expenses not covered by insurance, eyeglasses, teeth cleaning, X rays, etc. If you don't use all the money in the account by the end of the year, you forfeit what's left, so experts recommend you set aside 80 percent of your anticipated expenses. Another big benefit to these reimbursement accounts: Your full amount is available to you at any time during the year, regardless of how much you've paid in so far.

208

Health insurance is complex and the choices can be intimidating. Benefits consultants traditionally have been available only to large companies. However, Wilkinson Benefit Consultants (800-296-3030) helps individuals and small businesses sort through their options. The company earns no commissions, but after learning what type of coverage you want, it will search its data base and, for a fee, will provide you with the three lowest-cost plans.

209

The *Medicare Participating Physician/Suppliers Directory* for your area will tell you which physicians limit their fees to the amount approved by Medicare. It should be available at your local library. If not, call the Social Security Administration hot-line (800-772-1213) and ask for the toll-free number for the insurer that processes Medicare claims in your state. They can send you a directory.

MORTGAGES

210

Interest on a home mortgage is one of the few income tax deductions for loan interest that survives. Here are the restrictions: (1) The loan must be used to acquire or improve your home; (2) Acquisition indebtedness cannot be more than $1,000,000; (3) A home-equity loan, in addition to your mortgage, can be used for any purpose, but the cap on the loan amount is $100,000; and (4) The total of all mortgage debt cannot exceed the fair market value of your home.

211

Most homeowners choose a fixed-rate mortgage so they can lock in an overall interest rate and a fixed payment every month. However, a much lower "adjusted-rate mortgage"

(ARM) may save you money if you're going to stay in your house only a short time, say, three to four years. The typical ARMs don't rise more than two percentage points a year and six points over the life of the loan. (You should *not* refinance your mortgage to an ARM if your mortgage has only a few years to go. At that point, you're repaying mostly principal.)

212

A "balloon mortgage" gives you low payments for a few years, and then the entire loan comes due. Choose this kind of mortgage only if you're certain you'll move before the balloon explodes. Some people then refinance at an affordable rate, but others have had to sell their homes.

213

Should you choose a mortgage with the lowest fixed rate and more points (a point equals 1 percent of the loan) charged up front, or the higher rate with no points? That depends on how long you expect to own your house. Go with no points if you expect to sell your home and move on after a few years, but if you expect to stay five years or more, choose the lower rate.

214

The points you pay when you buy your house are deductible in full in the year you buy. However, to qualify for the deduction, the points must be paid out of your own funds rather than added to the mortgage loan. Write a check for the points at your closing.

215

If you make a down payment of less than 20 percent on your house, you probably will be required to have mortgage insurance, a monthly fee that protects the lender in case you default on the loan. But you don't have to pay indefinitely. Once you've paid off enough of the loan so the balance equals 80 percent or less of the value of your house, you can drop the insurance. Ask your lender at what loan-to-value ratio it will agree to release you from paying premiums.

216

Accelerate the payments on your mortgage and save. Not having to pay interest on a 9 percent mortgage is as good as earning 9 percent. Furthermore, it's cheaper to accelerate payments on your present mortgage if you have a reasonable interest rate and will really do it. Syndicated money columnist Jane Bryant Quinn offers this convincing example: If you have twenty years left to pay on a thirty-year loan of $100,000 and you add just $50 more a month to your payments, you'll own your home two years earlier and save $17,400 in interest costs.

217

One reason *not* to refinance is that when you begin a new mortgage loan, you're paying only interest (or mostly interest). If you've been paying on a mortgage for several years, you're paying back principal, and it will be costly to you in the long run to go back to square one.

218

Many homeowners have a fixed-rate mortgage plus a "home-equity credit line" whose interest rate floats at a certain percentage above prime. While interest rates are low, it may be prudent to refinance the total loan and lock in a lower fixed-rate (by lowering your monthly costs). Check with your accountant.

219

It makes sense, and saves money, to refinance a mortgage if the new fixed rate of loan interest is at least 2 percent lower than what you're currently paying. Another question to ask: Is the money you'll save on monthly payments equal to or more than the financing costs over two or three years? If the answer is yes, go ahead.

220

If you decide to refinance at a fixed rate, make sure your new mortgage lasts no longer than your old one. If you have twenty-five years to go and refinance for thirty years, you may not save any money because you'll add five more years of interest payments. Ask your lender how much you'll have to pay each month to retire the new mortgage in the years remaining on your old loan. If possible, make the new one even shorter.

221

When you refinance your mortgage, the IRS requires that you spread the points that you had to pay up front over the life of the loan. However, there's money to be saved if you use a portion of the loan to cover home improvements. In this case, the IRS says a portion of the points may be deductible for the year you paid them.

222

If you claimed extra withholding allowances based on your mortgage-interest deduction and then you refinance your loan, remember to check your W-4. If refinancing reduced the interest you pay, you may need to cut your number of allowances.

223

"The cheapest way to live in retirement is in a paid-up house," says syndicated money columnist Jane Bryant Quinn. She advocates that when you're forty years old, you should refinance and take a fifteen-year mortgage. "Your monthly payments may be higher, but over the long term, you'll save thousands in interest. And you'll own your own home when you're fifty-five."

224

"When you get or refinance any loan, have the lender spell out all the extra costs in writing," says my friend Denise, who learned this lesson the hard way when she refinanced her mortgage. "There can be more fees than a zebra has stripes. Unless you ask what they are, you won't be told until you're asked to pay them."

$$\boxed{225}$$

A "reverse mortgage" has been a very popular way to enhance retirement income. The home serves as collateral for monthly payments that are made to the homeowner, and then the loan is repaid from the estate of the borrower after his or her death. The most advantageous terms provide for payments to continue for the life of the surviving spouse.

MOVING

226

Move on a weekday. Fees can be as much as 50 percent higher on the weekend.

227

Pack everything yourself and save at least 10 percent. Most movers provide cartons for this.

228

Get a binding estimate in writing from your moving company *before* you move. In 24 percent of nonbinding estimates around the country, the actual cost of a move exceeds the estimate. A binding estimate will cost more, but the price is guaranteed.

229

If you haven't done it already, there's no better time to video-tape your belongings than before they're packed. Your tape will be an important document should you need to file an insurance claim later. Keep the tape with your other important papers and hand-carry all of them to your new destination and then immediately to a new safe deposit box.

230

If you are moving out-of-state and you visit your new location before moving your belongings, open a checking account. Otherwise, to cover your expenses for a couple of weeks, bring traveler's checks. You'll probably have to wait until you have an in-state driver's license before you can cash personal checks, and there could be a delay in receiving your new checks.

231

Hand-carry all your negotiable securities to your new safe deposit box. Make photocopies of all the documents so you'll have a record of the registration numbers, and mail them ahead.

232

Confirm with your insurance agent that you'll be covered for the possessions you move personally, beyond coverage you buy from a moving company. The items you take in your car are probably the most valuable. Coverage will be through your homeowners or renters policy, not your auto policy.

233

The 1993 tax law overhauled deductions for unreimbursed moving expenses in a job-related move. As of this writing, the only expenses you can still deduct are the costs of moving your household goods and personal effects and of traveling (lodging but *not* meals) to the new location. The only good news is you no longer have to itemize deductions in order to claim moving expenses.

234

You may deduct moving expenses from your gross income only if your new home is at least fifty miles away from your last residence than your old job was from your old home.

REAL ESTATE

235

You can avoid paying a Realtor's commission, very often 6 percent of the selling price, by marketing your home yourself. "All you need is a good ad in the right newspapers," says my friend Charles, a veteran of selling homes himself. "You also need a good lawyer and the time in your life to show the house to prospective buyers."

236

Architects frequently charge 20–40 percent of the cost of a building project. Tom and Carol built their own home, but they substantially reduced their costs by giving sketches of what they wanted to a building consultant, whose fee was only 10 percent. The consultant then hired a draftsman, at an hourly rate, to prepare the working drawings.

237

According to my friend Nancy, a successful Realtor, there are three essential steps to take if you want to make the most profit when you sell your home through a Realtor: (1) Price your house appropriately, (2) Make sure it's in pristine condition inside and out, and (3) Eliminate all clutter. "If your house hasn't sold in a month, lower the price," Nancy says. "The worst case is for a house to sit and sit and sit unsold."

238

Are you looking for a second home at a bargain price? As a result of the savings-and-loan crisis, the federally chartered Resolution Trust Corporation (RTC) has many resort properties for sale, in some cases, at half the original price. For information, call 800-431-0600.

239

To avoid costly surprises when you buy a new home, make sure your contract reads that your deposit will be returned if the inspection uncovers a major problem. Or, the buyer can stipulate that the seller will pay for the needed repairs or lower the purchase price. If the repairs cannot be completed before the closing, the seller must deposit money in an escrow account to cover the repair costs.

240

Some home sellers who want to get top dollar for their home have it inspected *before* they put it on the market. "This gives the seller time to correct any problems," says Jim, a Realtor. "And don't forget, cosmetic improvements you make to your home within six months before you sell it, so-called 'fixing-up expenses,' may be deductible."

241

"As long as you have the cash flow," says Martin, an accountant, "you may as well buy a big house with a big mortgage. Mortgage interest is one of the few tax deductions that Congress hasn't done away with, so enjoy your big home and enjoy keeping your money away from Uncle Sam."

242

Your most important job when selling your house is pricing it intelligently (as opposed to pricing it according to what profit you need). Get the opinions of three qualified Realtors. In addition to their idea of how to price your home, ask each Realtor what they would do to market it if they had the listing. The most advertising goes to the customers who agree to pay the largest commissions.

243

Most larger real estate firms give their agents an incentive to sell the company's own listings. Whereas an agent always benefits by contributing to any sale, he or she gets a larger commission when the company had the listing. As a home seller, you will get more attention from your listing firm's agents.

244

Attorney closing costs for buying or selling real estate are negotiable. If you're *buying* a property, in most areas the cost of title insurance is fixed, but you should shop around for attorney's fees. If a lawyer says he or she charges by the hour, know that the billing units are most always quarter hours; that is, if you converse for five minutes, you're charged one quarter of an hour. In my geographic area, this always costs the client more.

245

When deciding with whom to list your property for sale, you'll have the most exposure to the most agents if your Realtor participates in multiple listing services. There's a fee for this. Make sure you ask in which listing services they are planning to include your property.

246

If you know what questions to ask, you can spot a declining real estate market before you buy in. Find out how many housing permits have been issued in the past three years. Has the number dropped, stayed the same, or risen? Second, ask real estate agents about the number of sales versus the number of listings. If sales aren't keeping up with listings, prices will eventually decline.

247

Does your mortgage payment include an amount for insurance and property taxes? If so, your lender holds those funds in escrow until the bills are due. However, fourteen states require the lender to pay interest on those funds: California, Connecticut, Iowa, Maine, Maryland, Massachusetts, Minnesota, New Hampshire, New York, Oregon, Rhode Island, Utah, Vermont, and Wisconsin.

248

It used to be you had two choices: You could sell your property yourself or delegate the work to a full-service Realtor. Now there's a third option: a discount broker. Help-U-Sell, for example, is a national discounter with franchises in forty-one states (800-366-1177). In addition, there are regional discounters. Arrangements vary, but commissions are always lower and, typically, the seller holds the open house.

249

Every owner likes to have a low appraisal of their home so property taxes will be low, but watch out when you go to sell— a savvy buyer may say your high asking price is not in line with your low appraisal. Also, a low appraisal can spell trouble for your buyer when applying for a mortgage. Most banks will lend a buyer only 80 percent of the appraised value. If your buyer is planning to pay a standard 20 percent down payment, he or she will also have to pay the difference between 20 percent of the appraised value and 20 percent of the selling price. Always check your contract to see whether there's a clause outlining what will happen in the event of a low appraisal.

250

Do you need more space, but you can't afford a bigger house? Many people decide to remodel or add on. Depending on the project you choose and where you live, you can recoup more than 100 percent of your costs when you do so. According to *Kiplinger's Personal Finance Magazine,* an additional bathroom is by far your best investment, followed by a remodeled kitchen, then an added family room.

251

If your real estate agent finds you a mortgage through her computerized loan origination (CLO) system (which can cost $250 or more), be sure it includes data from the majority of institutions making loans in your area.

252

You don't need a real estate agent just to drive you to a model home and introduce you to a developer. He or she may agree to reduce the home sale price by a portion of the 6 percent fee that would otherwise be paid to an agent. However, if he or she won't budge in price, a buyer can often get significant upgrades in interior features.

253

Paying $300 to $500 for a home warranty is *not* a wise investment. Warranties are frequently filled with exclusions. You're
much better off spending your money on a reliable home inspection.

254

According to the National Association of Home Builders
(NAHB), the national median home price, as of October 1992,
was $110,000. Of the most affordable places to buy a home,
most were in the Midwest; the least affordable were in California. If you'd like to know the housing costs for any region
in the country, write to NAHB, Public Affairs, 1201 15th St.
NW, Washington, DC 20005-2800 (800-368-5242).

255

If your income is growing, and the same goes for home values
in your area, you may not have to sell your first home in order
to move on to the next. Take out a home equity loan and use
it as a down payment on your next house. Use your rental
income, usual mortgage money, and some additional income to
pay the mortgage on the second house and the equity loan on
the first. Now you have two assets appreciating in value.

REDUCING DEBT

256

Rick was laid off for six months and accumulated some debt on his charge cards. He was successful in eliminating what he owed by putting his cards in a drawer and not charging anything, by paying each company a little every month, and most important, by renegotiating a lower interest rate. "The point is you have to be pro-active," he says. "You have to go to them with a plan."

257

If you're trying to reduce your spending, don't trim your budget so close to the bone that you have no discretionary funds. Pay yourself and your other family members a modest "allowance" to spend as you wish. Your budget will be easier to stick to if you don't feel like you have to sacrifice everything, including small pleasures.

258

Credit card companies usually need cash. Furthermore, if you have a large, unpaid balance, they would rather not turn you over to a collection agency. A family I know responded to a one-time offer: "If you pay your full balance in thirty days, the company will accept 85 percent of the amount owed." Why not propose a similar solution to the companies you owe?

259

Budget counselors recommend that you consolidate loans at the lowest possible interest rate, which is generally a home-equity or credit union loan.

260

Mend your ways. After you have eliminated your debts, resolve not to incur them again. And make it a rule never to buy something in anticipation of income. You may get the income, but you forgot to *also* anticipate the boiler that breaks, the unreimbursable medical expense, or the major car repair.

261

Negative information can remain on a credit report for up to seven years; bankruptcy for ten. However, help is available from the Consumer Credit Counseling Service, which operates 750 offices across the country. It helps people set up a budget, understand their credit reports, and repay creditors. For the office nearest you, call 800-388-CCCS.

262

If you want to make certain you pay off your debts a little at a time, you can arrange for your bank to send a fixed amount to certain creditors every month. And if you request it, the bank will remind you in advance to deduct the payment from your balance.

263

Believe it or not, you will save money if you use your savings to pay off your debts. If you have a savings account earning 4 percent interest and a credit card costing 19 percent, you're losing 15 percent a year. It's better to use your savings to pay off the debt. Then make monthly payments into your savings account instead of to the credit card company.

SELF-EMPLOYMENT

264

Even after the 1986 Tax Reform Act, Congress preserved some tax advantages for small-business owners. For example, while interest on loans that are not secured by a mortgage on your home is no longer deductible from your income tax, if you own your own business, you can still deduct the interest on business loans.

265

If you are self-employed, your business travel expenses are *fully* deductible on Schedule C for Form 1040 for sole proprietorships, or on a partnership return. If you work for someone else,

50 percent of your *unreimbursed* meals is deductible. The rest of your unreimbursed travel expenses falls into "miscellaneous itemized deductions," which are allowed only to the extent they exceed 2 percent of your adjusted gross income.

266

To claim home-based business deductions, you must file Form 8829, Expenses for Business Use of Your Home, which is now required for anyone who files Schedule C, Profit and Loss from Business, with the 1040 form. Getting the most out of your business deductions is a matter of keeping detailed expense records, including receipts and canceled checks. You may not, however, deduct more than your net income, before the home office deduction.

267

To claim a home office deduction, the room(s) must be used exclusively and regularly as a place of business. Furthermore, if you have been *depreciating* your office, when you go to sell your home, the depreciation will lower your cost basis, which will result in higher profits and possibly a larger capital gain. Claiming home office expenses deserves close scrutiny by your accountant.

268

If you become disabled, disability income benefits are tax-free *unless,* as a corporation, you have been deducting the annual premiums. If you have your own business and are incorporated, resist the temptation to deduct those premiums. While you're actively working, you're much more financially able to skip the deduction. If you become disabled, you don't want the added burden of paying taxes on your benefits.

269

The 1986 Tax Reform Act did away with the first $100 of dividends that an individual could exclude from taxable income. However, if you are the owner of a corporation, you can take advantage of a 70 percent tax deduction on dividends. For your corporation, a good investment is a high-yielding investment such as preferred stock.

SHOPPING

270

According to the U.S. Department of Agriculture, from 1982 to 1992 the cost of all food rose 42 percent, and breakfast cereals alone rose 85 percent. However, my friend Nancy, a caterer, insists that while it may not be possible to beat the tide of inflation at the grocery store, you can slow it down a little. She recommends buying larger quantities (they cost less per pound), choosing the cheaper store brands whenever possible, and using coupons for the national brands that you prefer. (Delegate clipping and filing—organized by store aisle—to your kids.)

271

Buying "refills" helps the environment and lowers your costs at the supermarket. Fruit juice or laundry detergent refills, for example, cost much less than the products in their original containers.

272

Grocery co-ops are a lot of work, but you can cut your food bill by as much as 40 percent. Members save money by buying in bulk from cooperative warehouses. To find out which warehouse serves your area, write to the National Cooperative Business Association, 1401 New York Ave. NW, Suite 1100, Washington, DC, 20005 (202-638-6222). The warehouse can refer you to the nearest buying club.

273

My friend Sharon is a master at turning old clothes into money by selling to consignment shops. With one son and one daughter, she insists there are many lives left in their jeans, shirts, coats, and more. "Follow the rules of the consignment shop as to number and condition of items," she advises. "And you'll

profit more by delivering clothing that is clean and on hangers."
For a zip code list of shops nearest you, write to the National
Association of Resale and Thrift Shops, 157 Halsted St., Chi-
cago Heights, IL 60411.

274

It's a fact: Little girls' playclothes cost more than boys'. For
pants and tops, buy your daughter's casual togs in the boys'
department, where they cost less.

275

The General Services Administration of the U.S. government
has put together a booklet, *Guide to Federal Government Sales,*
which tells you how to take advantage of bargains at government auctions or sales of real estate, surplus, or confiscated
vehicles. To request your free copy, send your name and address to Consumer Information Center, Dept. 71, Pueblo, CO
81009.

276

The Consumer Information Center also publishes a catalog that
lists hundreds of free and low-cost federal publications on a
wide range of subjects. To order, see tip 275.

277

Know the full range of benefits from your professional association. You may be entitled to some discounts that you thought were available only to large companies. The National Federation of Press Women (NFPW), for example, has negotiated a contract with Penny Wise, the largest office products network in the nation. The NFPW program enables members to save an additional 4–11 percent off their already discounted prices.

278

Have you ever returned home with your purchase from the hardware store only to discover you already had the item tucked away in a remote corner? To avoid duplication of purchases, store items by height. If you can't see it, you don't know you have it.

279

According to the American Managed Care Pharmacy Association, mail-order drug sales will increase 33 percent this year. Mail-order pharmacies buy in bulk and therefore can get significant discounts from manufacturers, which they pass on to you. They also work to substitute cheaper brand-name equivalents or generic drugs. If you're over age fifty and a member of the American Association of Retired Persons (AARP), you can save money by using their mail-order pharmacy service. For information, call the AARP at 800-274-0344.

280

You can clothe yourself and your whole family with an average savings of 30–70 percent off retail by shopping at factory outlets, and a good guidebook can direct you there. *Outletbound: Guide to the Nation's Best Outlets* lists more than nine thousand factory-direct stores. For information or to order regional brochures, call 800-336-8853.

281

Some national guides to factory outlet stores, like *The Joy of Outlet Shopping*, include coupons worth more than $200. For information, call 800-344-6397.

282

Ask your favorite factory outlets and discount stores to put you on their mailing lists. With advance notice of special sales, you can realize bigger savings.

283

Save money by shopping at warehouse club stores. The Price Company and Costco Wholesale Corporation have merged into Price-Costco and are expanding their membership-club chains. For information on the warehouse nearest you, call 800-597-7423.

284

Shopping by mail all year, instead of all at once before the holidays, can prevent huge bills on your credit cards in January, along with the resulting interest charges if you take several months to pay them off. Keep a list of your friends and family, along with a specific budget for each person or occasion, and shop by mail every month. Keep the gifts hidden away or wrap them as they arrive. Come next December, sit back and watch everyone else in a holiday frenzy!

285

When my son was young but tall for his age, I could predict that his clothing size would be twice his age, that is, at six months he wore size twelve months, at one year, he wore 2 T, and so on. Knowing this, I often saved money by buying his clothes on sale in advance. However, children grow so fast in the early months and years that once or twice, I found myself with a warm jacket in July or shorts in January. Shop on sale, but watch out for the change in seasons!

286

Consumer buying clubs are popping up everywhere. In exchange for membership dues, they promise you the opportunity to buy from major suppliers at wholesale prices, just like the buyers for major department stores do. After receiving a telemarketing call, I visited one of these "clubs" to see their pitch. They *said* they had more than 500,000 members nationwide, they *said* they did business with hundreds of major "household word" manufacturers, but I saw nothing in writing. To join, I had to sign up then and there; I couldn't think it over and return. I declined. Moral? If you agree to hear a sales pitch like this, call your Better Business Bureau and learn all you can about the company *before* you go.

287

A subscription to *Freebies* magazine for $7.95 a year ($4.95 if you mention this book!), will keep you informed about free and inexpensive items available to anyone. Send a check to *Freebies*, P.O. Box 5025, Carpinteria, CA 93014-5025, (805-566-1225).

288

You can save a lot of money with some of the food and freezer plans that deliver to your home, but read the fine print of the contract carefully. Ask if there's an initial or annual membership fee. Also, very low prices are enticing, but do they include meat cutting, wrapping, and freezing? If you don't pay in advance, are you charged interest? And if the plan includes a freezer and you drop out of the plan, will you still have to pay for the freezer?

289

If you live near one of the 155 national forests, you may have access to up to six cords of free firewood. Check with your regional office of the U.S. Forest Service.

290

Very few people can take the time to read all the grocery and discount circulars that come in newspapers and then drive all over town purchasing the best deals. Some people choose to save time (and fuel) by shopping at only one nearby grocery for everything. There's probably a happy medium. Keep shopping lists for two or three stores—perhaps the discount drug store and discount department store, plus your favorite grocery. When you need six or more items from one place, it's time to make the trip.

291

When you ask your print shop to hurry, they charge you "rush" fees. To avoid these extra costs, insert "flags" that will signal to you that you're running low on printed materials—stationery, PR materials, applications, flyers, etc.—so you can order new supplies before you run out.

TAXES

292

If you itemize deductions, don't forget to deduct your "miscellaneous itemized deductions." These can include union dues, tax preparation fees, broker's fees, investment magazine subscriptions, transportation related to your investments, seminar and convention fees, and other expenses. However, these deductions are allowed only to the extent they exceed 2 percent of your adjusted gross income.

293

Believe it or not, there are still a few categories of income that are not included in gross income on your federal tax return: (1) life insurance proceeds that you receive when someone dies who named you as a beneficiary; (2) gifts that you receive or money that you inherit; (3) premiums paid by your employer on the first $50,000 of term life insurance; and (4) interest on tax-exempt state and local government bonds (although you must still report this interest and be subject to "alternative minimum tax").

294

When you donate appreciated securities—stocks, bonds, or mutual funds—that you've owned for more than a year, you claim the current market value as a charitable contribution and don't have to pay tax on the profit. For example, if you own a stock worth $10,000 that you purchased years ago for $2,500, selling your shares would give you a $7,500 taxable capital gain ($2,100 in a 28 percent bracket). If you give the stock away, there's no tax on the gain and you get to deduct the full $10,000. (However, the additional deduction may be subject to "alternative minimum tax.")

295

There are seven states that have no income tax—Alaska, Florida, Nevada, South Dakota, Texas, Washington, and Wyoming. In New Hampshire and Tennessee, rates apply to income from dividends and interest only. But before you relocate to one of these low-tax havens, there may be others costs to consider: property taxes, sales taxes, utility costs, insurance costs, etc. Right Choice, Inc., in Derry, New Hampshire, will send you a detailed analysis of a region, including all the expenses, taxes, and services you should be aware of before relocating. Call 800-872-2294.

296

If parents give money to their children, they shift income-producing assets to family members in lower tax brackets and reduce the size of their estate, and therefore, their estate taxes. As part of the federal gift-tax exclusion, anyone may give another person $10,000 a year, tax-free.

297

If you transfer legal title to an asset to your child, through either the Uniform Gift to Minors Act (applicable in twenty states) or the Uniform Transfer to Minors Act (in the other thirty states), don't name yourself as custodian of your own gifts. If you do and die before your child becomes an adult, the value of your gift will be taxed as part of your estate. Name your spouse or a third party instead.

298

There are two types of trusts that qualify for the annual gift-tax exclusion that you can set up for your children: a minor's, or 2503 (c) trust, and a Crummey trust. You'll need a lawyer to draw up the trust agreement. However, unless you're going to transfer assets of more than $50,000, it's not worth the $1,000 to $1,500 you'll pay in legal fees, or the annual accounting costs you'll pay for keeping records and filing trust income tax returns.

299

If you have substantial assets, another creative way to pass them to your children in your lifetime and avoid estate taxes is to set up a parent-child limited partnership. You and your spouse can then transfer to each of your children an interest in your home or business worth up to $20,000 every year. The advantage to these partnerships is parental control: You keep the property in your hands until you think your child is ready to handle it.

300

While state and local income taxes and property taxes are still deductible on your tax return, sales taxes are not. However, if you paid sales taxes on expensive items that are likely to increase in value, such as building materials for your home, jewelry, or art, save your receipts. When you sell the property, the sales tax you paid is considered part of your initial cost, and therefore will reduce the amount of your taxable profit.

301

You must pay attention to your investment portfolio, but especially just before December 1. Having a capital loss on your tax return might be the push you need to sell a losing venture. Losses first offset any gains for the year. Then, up to $3,000 of additional capital losses can be deducted against other kinds of income, including your salary.

302

What tax papers must you keep and what can you throw out? The basic rule is to keep whatever you would need to convince an IRS agent auditing your return that your figures are accurate. For the most part, however, the IRS can't audit you more than three years after the due date of your return (the IRS destroys returns after seven years). Information establishing the cost of investment assets you own needs to be kept until three years after you've disposed of the asset. The same goes for any property you're depreciating. If you make nondeductible IRA contributions, save Form 8606 until you empty all your IRAs.

303

In the late fall, many stock mutual funds announce their annual distributions of dividends and capital gains. To avoid paying tax on these distributions, time your fund purchases to come just after, instead of just before, the date on which the announcement is made.

304

Tax experts argue that anytime you get an income tax refund of $500 or more, the money could have been put to better use earning interest for you. True in theory, but the larger question to ask is: Are you a disciplined saver? If you adjust your withholding so you receive the extra money in your net pay, will you save it, or spend it? If you're more likely to spend the smaller amount along the way, then wait for your refund and save *that*.

305

Municipal bonds are *not* an appropriate investment for tax-deferred accounts, such as IRAs. The reason is that money you withdraw from that account at retirement will be considered taxable income, regardless of what it was invested in. So you would do better to put your money in a higher yielding, though taxable, investment.

306

When you pay your child's day-care center, save your receipts. You may be entitled to a federal tax credit of up to 25 percent, depending on your income. The credit is on expenses up to $2,400 for one child, and up to $4,800 for two or more children. Strict limitations apply, so be sure to check with the IRS or your accountant.

307

Mortgage interest and property taxes for a second home are fully deductible; points are deducted over the life of the loan. You can rent your home, and not claim the rent as income, and still take the deductions. The rules change, however, if you rent your property for fifteen days or more. Avoid costly mistakes by consulting your accountant.

308

Job-hunting expenses are deductible if you itemize. Keep track of what you pay for printing and mailing resumes, phone calls, and employment agency fees. If you have to travel for interviews, you can also write off 80 percent of what you pay for food, lodging, and transportation. There is a restriction, however: These costs are considered "miscellaneous itemized deductions," so you may deduct only the amount that exceeds 2 percent of your adjusted gross income.

309

Be careful about claiming casualty losses on your tax return. You can reduce your adjusted gross income by the amount of casualty losses to your property, but only after you've filed an insurance claim. Also, the amount of your loss has to be reduced by what you collect from your insurance company. And finally, casualty losses above $100 are deductible only to the extent that they exceed 10 percent of your adjusted gross income.

310

If you change jobs or lose your job, resist the temptation to take retirement money as current income. There's now a mandatory 20 percent federal tax withholding if you don't roll the money over directly into a new plan or IRA, plus a 10 percent penalty if you're under age 59 and one half. The best ways to handle a lump-sum payout are: (1) Roll it over into your next employer's pension plan; (2) Put it into an Individual Retirement Account (IRA) at a bank or mutual fund; or (3) Leave it with your ex-employer to manage. (See tip 198.)

311

If you want to avoid paying someone to prepare your income tax returns and you own a personal computer, buy and install one of the inexpensive software programs such as Tax Cut or Turbo Tax to get the job done.

312

To claim a deduction on your income tax for charitable contributions other than cash totaling more than $250—furniture to the rummage sale, clothes to the thrift shop, a piece of silver to the church auction—the IRS says the assigned value must be determined by the charity. Since few charities have enough volunteers to assign values to contributions, you should list each item with an appropriate resale price and ask the charity to put its stamp on it. If your noncash contributions come to more than $5,000, there's a different procedure. Check with your accountant.

313

Are you feeling burdened by large property-tax payments on your home? Call your tax collector and ask if your state or local government will allow you to defer your payments until you die or your house is sold. Nineteen states and the District of Columbia provide this kind of relief by placing a tax lien against your property and charging interest on the taxes that accrue.

314

When you employ a nanny to care for your children, or other domestic help, you must pay a Social Security tax of 15.3 percent, which is sent quarterly to the IRS on Form 942. You owe half and your nanny owes half. If you pay her share, you have to report that amount as additional wages. You also have to file a W-2 form showing total wages paid. Or, you can delegate all this red tape to Paychex, Inc., in Rochester, New York (800-322-7292). For about $1 per week, Paychex will pay your employee and handle all the withholding and government filing. Paychex operates in eighty-seven locations nationwide and assumes full responsibility for accuracy.

315

Tax credit investments are one of the few true tax shelter investment opportunities available today. By buying participation in a portfolio of investments in low-income housing, you receive tax credits and a 15 percent after-tax return for the first ten years, plus the opportunity for capital back after a fifteen-year holding period. The minimum investment is $5,000, with increments of $1,000, up to an individual limit of $50,000. Investors have an opportunity to offset tax each year on up to $25,000 of non-passive income. Tax credit investments are sold through major brokerage houses.

TELEPHONES

$$\boxed{316}$$

Comparing long-distance telephone services causes my eyes to glaze over. However, if you want to reduce your current phone bill, you can contact companies at their toll-free numbers:

Allnet	800-783-2020
AT&T	800-222-0300
Metromedia	800-275-2273
MCI	800-444-3333
Sprint	800-877-4000

Or you can send a stamped, self-addressed envelope and $2 to the Telecommunications & Action Center, P.O. Box 12038, Washington, DC 20005 (202-462-2520). They will send you extensive, updated comparisons of the various long-distance plans.

317

Buy your own telephones. I confess that for many years, I continued to rent two telephones in my home (while owning two others). Finally, I returned them to the phone company and replaced them with quality models. The money I saved from no longer renting paid for my new phones in less than a year.

318

A low-cost answering machine is still the most economical way to receive messages while you're away from the office or home. However, the new voice mails offered by phone companies—with names like Personal Secretary and Answer Call—offer some advantages not available from the traditional machines and can save you a lot of time. With extra codes, you can have several message boxes. You can also "mail" a recording to selected phone numbers, which is useful if you need to alert several people of a new meeting time or place. At just $10 for installation, and $5 to $7 a month to use, these services deserve a look.

319

If you use a facsimile ("fax") machine, you can save money by programming your fax to "auto-dial" and send your documents after 5:00 P.M., or when long-distance rates are cheaper.

320

Judy, who works at home, put her fax line on her children's phone line. "A business line costs more than a children's number. Also, my teenagers are in school or at after-school activities during business hours when I send and receive faxes. My kids usually return home after 5:00 P.M. when the fax line is free for their use."

321

Sending a fax can cost less than first-class postage; that's pennies. However, "time is money," and sending a fax takes a lot less time than engaging in a lengthy phone conversation; that's dollars.

322

Sending written documents via computer modem can be even less expensive than transmitting by fax. You save paper and labor, in that the receiver doesn't have to word-process or re-design your material. It's transmitted from screen to screen.

323

Did you know you don't need a separate telephone line for your fax machine? All fax machines currently sold have an automatic fax-phone switch.

324

If you have two or more telephone lines in your home or office, you don't need to pay for "call waiting" service. A free feature of your second line is that if one line is busy, it "hunts" for the second.

TRAVEL

325

Two families renting a large vacation house can save more money than if they rented two homes separately. Sara and David found a shortage of two-bedroom seaside cottages, but when they decided to combine forces with another family—one week first family alone, one week together, one week second family alone—they had more choices of rentals, much grander quarters, and saved on the per week cost.

326

A young couple with two children sat down to brainstorm not only ideas for their next family vacation destination but also how they were going to save for it. Their unanimous decision was to drink water at restaurants instead of the more costly soft drinks and milk shakes. By sacrificing their preferred beverages during a once-a-week restaurant outing, the family could afford their annual summer vacation.

327

One of the most satisfying ways to appreciate your tax dollars at work is to visit the museums of the Smithsonian Institution in Washington, D.C. Admission is free to the Freer Gallery of Art, the Hirshhorn Museum and Sculpture Garden, the Museum of African Art, the National Museum of Natural History, the National Air and Space Museum, the National Museum of American Art, the National Portrait Gallery, and the Renwick Gallery.

328

One couple I know whose budget is tight arranges a weekend alone several times a year by having their kids stay overnight with another family. Mom and Dad go out for dinner but save on hotel costs by sleeping at home. Later on, they reciprocate by having the other couple's kids for a weekend.

329

Always pay for travel—hotels, transportation, rental cars, etc.—by credit card. If you pay by check and your service is not satisfactory, you've lost your money. With a credit card, you don't have to pay the bill for poor service.

330

You can often slash the cost of hotels, rental cars, and other travel arrangements by booking an independent package from a tour operator. No groups or guides come with the deal, just lower rates negotiated by the operator. Some packages may simply yield a discounted hotel or rental-car price, but others, such as Caribbean and ski packages, may include airfare and accommodations for less than the published room rates at the same resorts. Check the ads in your newspaper's travel section.

331

Last Minute Travel Connection offers up-to-the-minute listings of leftover bargains on air fares, hotels, condominiums, cruises, and packaged tours. To use their service, call 900-446-8292. The call costs $1 per minute, with the average call lasting three to five minutes.

332

Traveling to warmer climes costs more during peak travel season, (for example, December 15 through April 30). You'll save money by traveling in the off-season, but "Who wants to go to Florida in July?" you ask. There's another option: "shoulder season," (typically December 1 through 15 for Florida and other points south) when rates cost more than "off" but less than "peak."

333

Consolidators, travel companies that buy up many airline tickets and/or many hotel rooms, get reduced rates from their volume purchase, which they then pass on to the consumer. You'll find their bargain prices in the travel section of your daily newspaper.

334

Travelers as young as age fifty qualify for senior hotel and car-rental discounts through the American Association of Retired Persons. It costs $8 a year to join (202-434-2277).

335

From *Best Fares: The USA Report* you can learn of dozens of airline, hotel, car-rental, and other travel discounts, with a city-by-city listing of the cheapest fares. An annual subscription costs $58 (800-880-1234).

336

TravelAlert (800-822-2300), a computerized data base, lists up to 850 discounts a day for cruises, hotels, tours, and other travel activities.

337

You can often save money by calling an individual hotel, rather than the 800 telephone number for the chain, and asking about local promotion rates. For example, I found three national hotels in Boston featuring weekend specials for the Boston Marathon, but the toll-free headquarters had no knowledge of the bargain packages.

338

When you attend business conferences, very often the conference fee is less if you book early. The same can be true with hotel reservations. When making your plans in advance, always ask your hotel, "Do you have an early-booking discount?" One possible downside to prepaid hotel and resort packages: You could forfeit the cost of your stay if you cancel. Be sure to ask!

339

If you're going to be staying at several locations during a trip, consider the convenience of discount vouchers, sold by travel agents and accepted at hotels nationwide. Sheraton and Holiday Inn are among the chains with prepaid voucher programs.

340

To fill up their rooms, hotels will sometimes give you a discount for booking a room at the last minute. If you find yourself changing or making new plans, always ask the hotel clerk if they have a last-minute booking discount. It's also possible they will upgrade your room for no additional charge.

341

In the summer and during school holidays, many colleges and universities offer accommodations at very low rates ($10 per person and up). For a complete listing, consult *Peterson's Directory of College Accommodations* by Jay Norman.

342

For more than ten years Marriott Hotels have had their Honored Guest Awards program, in which frequent guests can earn free vacations at the chain's 250 properties. Marriott also offers Marriott Miles, where guests earn mileage credits for an airline ticket. You have to sign up for the awards programs separately, and when you check into a hotel you must specify whether you want to earn mileage or points towards a vacation. Enrollment forms are available at Marriott hotel front desks, or you can sign up by calling 800-367-6453.

343

A number of U.S. hotel chains and car-rental companies offer frequent-flier credits when you check in. These programs start up and disappear frequently, so be sure to check with your favorite airline, hotel chain, and car-rental firm for a list of partners and awards, and keep an eye open for mail announcements of special double- or triple-mileage promotions.

344

If you travel often, it pays to belong to a half-price hotel program. Entertainment Publications (800-477-3234) produces a variety of directories that list hundreds of hotels, restaurants, and attractions that offer discounts. Subscribers get 50 percent off hotel rates or 10 percent off promotional rates.

345

To pick up the best car-rental rates, become a regular reader of your Sunday newspaper's travel section. The best deals are short-term promotions that aren't even in a firm's reservations system. To take advantage, you must quote a code from the ad.

346

As a general rule, daily rental-car rates are highest, weekend and weekly rates the lowest. Since add-ons, surcharges, and taxes can double the quoted cost of a rental, ask the agent to calculate your total cost before you drive off.

347

Consider driving someone else's car to your vacation destination. Auto transport companies (listed in the Yellow Pages) are often looking for good drivers to drive cars from one part of the country to another. You pay only for gas.

348

By now most people know the restrictions on the lowest domestic airfares: Book your seat and buy your ticket well in advance, fly midweek, and stay over Saturday night. In addition, ask about flights that leave earlier or later than your first choice, as well as about connecting fares, which can be cheaper than flying direct or nonstop.

349

If you can't stay over Saturday night, try pricing two round-trip tickets, each meeting the requirement for the lowest fare. Flying out on one ticket and returning home on another can actually cost less than a single undiscounted round-trip.

350

You can often pick up a reduced-fare airline ticket by paying close attention to your newspaper's classified ads. When someone's travel plans change, he or she will try to sell, at a lower cost, a transferable certificate. In addition, some of the greatest discounts are available from frequent-flier-coupon brokers or by purchasing "hidden city" tickets (you're booked to a distant city but get off the plane at a more expensive stop en route). Look for bargains under "airlines," "travel," etc.

351

Your travel-date choices will be limited, but there are big savings to be had if you sign on as a free-lance air courier, someone who carries documents or small packages for a business. For more information, call the International Association of Air Travel Couriers in Lake Worth, Florida (407-582-8320), or Now Voyager in New York City (212-431-1616).

352

The latest trend in low-cost air travel is a public charter. This means that companies like Skybus, Carnival Air Lines, Private Jet, and Morris Air lease planes and flight crews for its flights. The lowest fare is for people who don't make reservations; in-flight meals, checking baggage, and a reserved seat cost more.

353

If your schedule is flexible and you aren't in a hurry to fly to your destination, be one of the passengers who volunteers to get off a flight that's overbooked. Your reward: a generous travel voucher or free round-trip ticket.

354

Actuaries, those mathematical types that calculate risks, say that you are fifty-six times more likely to be killed in an accident while in a car than in a plane. Since you don't take out extra insurance every time you get in a car, why purchase flight insurance when you travel by air?

UTILITIES

355

When it's time to buy an electric appliance, pay attention to the EnergyGuide label, mandated by the federal government, which tells you how the unit compares to others in the same category for energy efficiency and yearly operating cost. Air conditioners are labeled with an EER (energy-efficient ratio) or SEER (seasonal energy-efficiency ratio). Be aware that while one unit with a superior rating may cost you more up front, it may save you money in energy costs over the lifetime of the appliance.

356

If you're remodeling your kitchen, keep in mind that you want to position your refrigerator so that cool air circulates around the coils. Researchers have found that efficiency falls as temperatures behind your refrigerator rise.

357

Buying an energy-efficient home may actually allow you to afford a more expensive home—by qualifying for a larger, "energy-efficient mortgage" (EEM). The borrower in effect adds the cost of energy measures to the mortgage, but the net effect is to reduce home ownership costs. National EEM programs are available through the Federal Housing Administration (FHA), the Department of Veterans Affairs (VA), and the Farmers Home Administration (FmHA).

358

What does energy efficiency cost, and how much energy will it save? The answers are often available at no cost, or low cost, from your utility company. A thorough energy audit should recommend specific efficiency measures for your home and should identify the most cost-effective measures. Be sure the auditor explains how the cost of improvements will be paid back in energy savings, which turns your cost into an *investment*.

359

Do you know the recommended R-value (insulation efficiency) for your geographic area? Owens/Corning has a booklet for homeowners that explains insulation terms and gives advice for do-it-yourselfers. To get your copy, call 800-GET-PINK.

360

A 60-watt incandescent (i.e., the kind you've known for years) light bulb burning for 10,000 hours (at the national average electricity rate) will cost you $57.50. One of the new fluorescent bulbs burning for the same time will cost $33.04. The new bulbs cost more, but they are much more energy efficient because they last ten times as long. Fluorescent bulbs are available at several hardware and discount department store chains, and many utilities sell them at a substantial discount.

361

It's far more *efficient* to use a light bulb of a lower wattage than to dim a high-wattage bulb. Nevertheless, a dimmer can extend the life of your bulb.

362

You'll reduce your electric bill if you put low-watt bulbs in lamps that are not used for reading. However, where you do need strong light, a 150-watt bulb is more efficient than two 75-watt bulbs.

363

Does your power company feature two-tier pricing? If it does, electricity usually costs less at night. Therefore, run your washer, dryer, dishwasher, or the self-cleaning cycle of your oven in the evening, when utility rates are lower.

364

Having a hard time convincing your spouse you need a microwave oven? Tell him or her that microwaves cook small servings with less than half the energy of electric ranges.

365

If you replace your old toilet with one of the new, low-flow varieties that uses 1.6 gallons per flush, you automatically and permanently reduce your household water consumption by 25 percent. Otherwise, pick up one of the toilet dam kits that shrinks the water used per flush from five to three gallons. That's a 40 percent savings every time you flush.

Dear Reader:

If you have some proven ways to save money, please let me hear from you. Write to me at Hearst Books, William Morrow & Company, Inc., 1350 Avenue of the Americas, New York, NY 10019.

Thank you.

Sincerely,
Lucy H. Hedrick

INDEX

Tip numbers follow index entries.

Index

bonds (*cont.*)
  individual, 151
  long-term vs. short-term, 164
  mini, 156
  municipal, 154, 155, 157, 305
  in mutual funds, 157, 167, 170
  Series EE United States savings,
    160, 162
  taxes and, 155, 159, 165, 166
  timing transactions in, 152, 163
  zero coupon, 153
bondswapping, 165
building consultants, 236
Business & Professional Women's
  Foundation, 53

"call waiting," 324
cameras, 13, 14, 15
cancer insurance, 203
capital gains or losses, 96, 169, 172,
  174, 267
car dealers, 16, 20, 22, 24
car insurance, 101–113
  age discount for, 117
  antitheft devices and, 110
  cellular phones and, 113
  children's, 105, 111
  collision coverage in, 103, 104
  deductible in, 19, 103
  driving record and, 108
  lawsuit limitations and, 105
  mileage and, 102
  rental-car, 112
car loans, 18, 35, 36, 43, 100
cars, 16–43, 100
  air conditioners in, 25, 37
  alarm systems in, 42
  bargaining for, 26, 29, 32
  best times to shop for, 26
  cash rebates on, 31
  cassette tapes for, 66
  corporate credit cards and, 69, 73
  cut-price model, 30
  energy costs of, 23

  European, bought in Europe, 16
  extended service contracts for, 37
  leased, 43
  maintenance of, 33, 34
  new-car sales tax on, 20
  painted surfaces of, 21
  paying cash for, 18
  quality of, 34
  rental, 112, 345, 346
  resale value of, 17, 20, 22
  self-servicing of, 33
  special features on, 17, 109
  stereo equipment in, 38–41
  theft of, 38–41, 110
  time required for stopping by, 19
  used, 28, 37
  used, sale by owner of, 17, 21, 22
car-shopping services, 27
Cash for College (McKee), 49
cassette tapes, 66
cellular phones, 113
certificates of deposit (CDs), 11, 87,
  166, 170, 182
certified Financial Planner (CFP),
  90
charitable remainder trust (CRT),
  96
charities, 75
checking accounts, 1, 3, 4, 6, 8, 12,
  230
Checks in the Mail, 1
children, 143, 300, 320, 326
  car insurance for, 105, 111
  saving under name of, 47
child support, 82
Citibank credit cards, 74
clothing, 273, 274, 280, 285
college, 44–53
  federal loans for, 50
  life insurance and, 137
  Series EE U.S. savings bonds
    and, 159
  travel accommodations in, 341
  tuition costs of, 48
  see also scholarships, college

Index

171

Index

Index

Index

Index

Norman, Jay, 341
Now Voyager, 351

"100 Highest Yields," 9
Orville Redenbacher's Second Start
    Scholarship Program, 53
Outletbound: Guide to the Nation's
    Best Outlets, 280

package tours, 330
paints, 143
parent-child limited partnership,
    299
Paychex, Inc., 314
Penny Wise, 277
Peterson's Directory of College
    Accommodations (Norman),
    341
power of attorney, 199
professional associations, shopping
    through, 277
proof sheets, photographic, 13
property taxes, 247

Quinn, Jane Bryant, 52, 216, 223
Quotesmith Corporation, 97

RAM Research, 76
real estate, 120, 235–255
  see also homes; home sales
realtors, 235, 237, 242, 243, 252
  discount brokers, 248
  multiple listing services of, 245
refills, 271
refrigerators, 356
Resolution Trust Corporation
    (RTC), 238
retirement, 137, 141, 142, 153, 182,
    201, 223, 225, 305
reverse mortgage, 225
Right Choice, Inc., 295

R-12 (Freon) refrigerant, 25
R-value (insulation efficiency),
    359
Rukeyser, Louis, 93

sales taxes, 20, 30
savings, 304, 326
  for college, 47, 52
savings accounts, 2, 3, 9, 12, 150,
    167, 197, 263
scholarships, college:
  eligibility for, 46
  merit, 49
  for older students, 53
  outside aid in, 45
  taxes and, 44
second homes, 238, 255, 307
Securities and Exchange
    Commission, 89
SelectQuote, 130
self-employment, 264–269
  in home-based business, 119,
    264, 266, 267, 320
shopping, 270–291
  for clothing, 273, 274, 280, 285
  consignment shops and, 273
  at government auctions, 275
  grocery, 270, 271, 272, 288,
    290
  through professional associations,
    277
Smithsonian Institution, 327
Social Security, 85, 209
  tax, 314
state income taxes, *see* income
    taxes, state
stocks, 179–191, 193, 269
  automatic reinvestment in, 183
  for college savings, 52
  insiders, heavily owned by, 181
  price-to-earnings (P/E) ratios of,
    181, 189
  recommended, 191
  split, 190

Index